Narrat...g

Narrating the Past

Fiction and Historiography in Postwar Spain

David K. Herzberger

Duke University Press

Durham and London

1995

© 1995 Duke University Press

All rights reserved

Printed in the United States of America on acid-free paper ∞

Designed by Cherie H. Westmoreland

Typeset in Fournier by Keystone Typesetting, Inc.

Library of Congress Cataloging-in-Publication Data appear

on the last printed page of this book.

For Benjamin and Jeffrey

Contents

❀

Preface

In the summer of 1975, while doing research in Madrid, I watched then President Gerald Ford and Francisco Franco ride together down the main avenue of the city. The large crowd that had gathered for the event was in a festive mood, and as the open car in which the two heads of state were riding approached the spot where I stood, the buzz of the crowd grew louder. It struck me at the time that the entire scene seemed out of phase with contemporary life, that nearly one hundred thousand Spaniards could not possibly be lifting their arms in the Fascist salute to praise Franco, that their singing of "Cara al sol" (the Fascist anthem) could not be more than an echo of another period of history. I was of course wrong. Franco and his regime had insinuated itself into the very heart of Spanish culture and had managed in a relatively short period of time to define the nature of life in postwar Spain.

As I continued to study the culture of Francoist Spain over the next decade, it became increasingly evident to me that the rule of Franco represented not only an important period within Spanish history, but that the Franco government also played a determining role in how we had come to understand Spanish history as a whole. It also became clear that the way in which the Regime had positioned itself within historical time grew from a desire to make the past the exclusive property of the State. In large part, historians of the Regime had succeeded in silencing dissident voices within their own ranks as well as in the intellectual community as a whole. Their tight grip on the past was sustained in part by censorship, but to a much larger degree by their authority over the teaching of history and over the methods and tenor of scholarly inquiry that appeared in professional journals and scholarly books.

I began my study of fiction and historiography in the late 1980s, after having many conversations with Spanish novelists about Franco and his hold over Spanish history. While nearly all of these novelists (e.g., Luis Goytisolo, Jesús Fernández Santos, Juan Benet, Camilo José Cela, Carmen Martín Gaite) agreed that the Spanish past often seemed pertinent to their writing, they could not, however, pin down how their works might be viewed as "historical." Certainly, Spanish novelists who grew to maturity during the Franco years cannot be tied to a unified manner of writing, nor can their work be reduced to a single focal point of dissent from the Regime. Their novels are richly diverse and complex, and it would diminish their significance to define them narrowly. But within the fiction of many Spanish writers during the Franco years there frequently exists a compelling desire to confront Francoist Spain and to scrutinize the Spanish past. When novels of these writers are read within the context of Francoist historiography, it is possible to discern an opposing view of the past and of how the past ought to be written about. These oppositions are the subject of this book.

Part of the research for this project was supported by the Research Foundation of the University of Connecticut and by a Provost's Research Fellowship, which enabled me to write major portions of this study. I wish to thank the university for its generous support of my work.

I am also grateful for the insightful readings of portions of my manuscript by my friends and colleagues, in particular Robert Spires, John Margenot, and Malcolm Compitello. Their understanding of contemporary Spanish fiction has helped make this a better book. During the past few years I have given several talks on history and fiction in Spain. The questions and discussion periods that followed often helped to shape my ideas and, in some cases, made me rethink them completely. It is therefore no small debt of gratitude that I owe to lively debate with colleagues and students as this project developed over the past five years. And finally, I have been blessed with the support of my family in this undertaking, especially of my wife Sharon, who read significant portions of the book and who always offered wise counsel. Any shortcomings and ambiguities that remain are of course my own responsibility.

Parts of chapters 2, 3, and 5 have appeared in article form in *Hispanic Review, PMLA,* and *Revista Hispánica Moderna,* respectively. I wish to express my thanks to the publishers for their permission to use this material here.

A Note on Translations

Unless indicated otherwise, English quotations from the following works are from the translations listed here: Juan Benet's *Volverás a Región (Return to Región,* trans. Gregory Rabassa, 1985); Benet's *Una meditación (A Meditation,* trans. Gregory Rabassa, 1982); Carmen Martín Gaite's *El cuarto de atrás (The Back Room,* trans. Helen Lane, 1983); Camilo José Cela's *San Camilo, 1936 (San Camilo, 1936,* trans. John H. R. Polt, 1991). See "Works Cited" for full publication information. All other translations are my own.

Introduction

Narrative Intimacies:

Fiction and History

—You are a man of books.

—A little so.

—What books have you read?

—History, Divinity, *Belles-letters.*

—What is the characteristic of history?

—Fiction.

—Of Novels?

—Truth.

—Hugh Brackenridge, *Modern Chivalry* (1792)

The writing of history during the Francoist rule of Spain (1939–1975) is a profoundly unsettling activity. I do not mean this in a positive sense—that a rich and open discussion among historians compelled the Franco regime to question its place and significance within the flow of Spanish history. Nor can it be said that a deep intellectual curiosity about the past nourished a debate between advocates of one perspective or another in an attempt to reconcile postwar antipathies. "Unsettling" here alludes to the recurrent and unresolvable tensions embedded in all attempts to write the past into being (the tensions of agency, power, and narrative perspective, for example), as well as to the specific paradoxes that arise when history and fiction together make contending (and contentious) claims upon the past. In post–Civil War Spain, authority over history is bound up with restrictive narrative practices shaped and regulated by historians of the State. The absence of choices and alternatives for framing the past therefore begets a narrowly construed notion of historical truth. This truth stands as a cutting denial of diversity and difference, and offers instead a legitimation of authenticity based upon the sheer force of political and discursive power.

The unsettling nature of writing history in postwar Spain, however, is more salutary than it might first appear. For many novelists, indeed, it insinuates the capacity of discourse to open narration to difference and to deepen the resonances of dissent. The telling of multiple stories to enhance what Walter Benjamin refers to as the utilitarian component of history (the giving of counsel for future understanding) is thus seen as crucial. History always resists narration, but the very precariousness of all narrative endeavors is both the source of historical vitality and the catalyst for historical explorations. Viewed in this light, the past springs forth as liquefied matter able to flow into one narrative structure or another, changing shape and meaning as it forms and reforms itself in unending patterns of deviance. Writing the past thus becomes a twofold endeavor: it is a way to write and to act against the grain, as well as a means to develop narrations that allow (and even compel) the opening of history to divergence. Matters of truth, meaning, and time (and, in this instance, the correlative issue of intellectual dissonance) are of course implicitly held up to scrutiny in all narrations. In Francoist Spain, however, they stand resolutely at the core of discourse as crucial determinants of authority over the past. While historiographers of the Regime seek to squeeze history into a tightly constructed and monologically defined set of narrative strategies, writers of fictions are able to controvert these strategies and assert dissonance through a normative set of principles of their own.

It is important to point out, however, that the relationship between history and fiction that I wish to establish here does not derive from either origin or intention. I am not seeking to prove, for example, that novelists set out to write the past (or to write *about* the past) with history books at their side, urged on by a desire to refute the official story. This occasionally may have occurred (Juan Benet offers a striking example, as I discuss in chapter 4), but it is largely incidental to my critical inquiry. While in theory a text consists of the forms and meanings of a mosaic of previous texts unnamed and unnameable, in critical practice the crossreading of texts calls forth specific impositions: new meanings are revealed, historical filiations discerned, and structural similarities laid bare across works that readers *choose* to summon forth. For the most part, therefore, the associations between history and fiction that I detect emerge from the practical matter of *reading* one form of narrative against another. Within this context, fiction is discerned above all as narration that affirms its authority over time. But as I point out, rather than draw its referent from history (the so-called facts of the matter), fiction reaches into time through the *discourse* of history (historiography) in order to subvert the narrative principles upon which the telling of that history is premised.

The principal focus of this study, then, is the relationship between historiography and fiction in Francoist Spain. But to articulate the focus is to draw forth as well powerful obstacles, since it has long been suggested (both by academic tradition and what might be termed "common sense") that the writing of history and the writing of fiction are largely different types of intellectual activity.[1] These differences are of course institutionally sanctioned: academic departments at colleges and universities are drawn so as to confirm the distinction clearly; professional societies enhance the separation of the two disciplines through their network of journals and conferences; students pursue academic majors and graduate degrees in one field or the other. Furthermore, historians in recent decades have attached themselves to the larger body of social sciences, while literary scholars have generally affirmed the humanistic exigency of their work even as they have sought to broaden its reach.

The commonsense arguments for sustaining difference are similarly familiar. They generally distinguish between intention and content in history and fiction as well as the received set of expectations about what each actually *does*. History, it is argued, reports on events that have occurred in real life and pursues the truth of the past through the objectifying sanctions of human knowledge. Fiction, on the other hand, relates imaginary events through the oxymoronic paradigm inherent in all storytelling of "it was and it was not." This is such an obvious difference between the two disciplines, and such a dramatic one as well, that it makes reconciliation beyond the merely superficial appear futile. Even when fiction steps outside the purely imaginary to embrace real events and people located in particular places and times, common sense most often prescribes that verification be sought elsewhere. If we wish to know how much or what particular aspect of a fiction is true (i.e., did it "really" happen that way?), we generally search for answers in the texts of historians, whose project turns upon truth and accuracy. In other words, it is commonly held that the function and value of history are closely allied with the real, and that history generally claims authority to uncover the truth of the past and to show its pertinence to the present.[2] In contrast, fiction in its most redemptive role opens the world to diversity and seeks to empower the invented, but is rarely called upon to validate past events and grant them authenticity within the flow of human time.

On the other hand, many scholars have argued in recent years that history and fiction bear similar marks of identity.[3] These marks are not free of ambiguity, nor even of contradiction, but they are shaped by a shared determinateness that prescribes the principles of coincidence between the two disciplines. It can be shown, for example, that the representational underpinnings of the real (history) and the imaginary often share the same points of reference. Hence it is possible to corroborate the reality-bearing component of both fiction and history through reference to chronicles, documents, photographs, and the like. In other words, some component parts of fiction and history are actually known and verifiable, even though separated from our immediate perception by time and space. These are the so-called facts of existence which, as Louis Mink suggests, "[stand] over against us, accepting our apperception of them but resisting incursion and manipulation" (94).[4] Within this view, the ontological standing of these facts appears unassailable, and their proper appearance before us is assured by the representational adequacy of language. Even a deconstructionist such as Jacques Derrida, whose project is to disrupt representational adequacy, seems unable to rid himself of facts found "out there" in the world. These facts are of course appropriated by a voice and conveyed through words, but nonetheless they retain a status beyond words. As Derrida puts it, "It is totally false to suggest that deconstruction is a suspension of reference. . . . [T]o distance oneself from the habitual structure of reference, to challenge or complicate our common assumptions about it, does not amount to saying that there is *nothing* beyond language" (Kearney 123–24).[5]

Beyond the mimetic residue of referentiality, however, the argument for similarity between history and fiction has been made most forcefully by poststructuralist critics and postmodern novelists, who have set out to collapse the traditional generic boundaries of discourse. As E. L. Doctorow avers, "There's no more fiction or nonfiction, there's only narrative" (Lowenthal 227). Such writers generally deny the referential truth of discourse, which traditionally has asserted meaning as the coequal of representation, and they speculate on the contingency of narrative as a sort of black adiaphane leavened by the dispersive elements of polysemy, (con)textualization, and the protean resonances of reader reception. Postmodern writers and critics suggest that to write past time into discourse (in both fiction and history) is always an act of deferral. There is no single truth that lies at the end of narration, only other truths repositioned within the narrative process. This notion is equally true from the standpoint of the reader. Since readers generally come to know the past when it has already been organized in one way or another (analytically, statistically, discursively, etc.), questions posed by readers have the potential to reorganize the received knowledge and reconstitute what is "given" into new patterns of sense. Pluralism and difference thus become the markers of all discourse (including history's). Even when one meaning projects a discursive authority that appears to embody truth, new textualizations and different configurations (offered by new writers and readers) implicate other truths, which engender others, and so on, until all boundaries of genre and all objective truths become merely the debris of the shattered referential illusion.

Theorists such as Hayden White and Paul Ricoeur, whose writing remains unattached to post-isms but whose intellectual reach extends through philosophy and human consciousness, have also sought to blend the lines of narration that define difference in history and fiction through a form of narrative "scumbling." The concept of scumbling is critical to conjoining historiography and fiction, though it is perhaps most fully realized in enterprises such as modern painting, where colors often bleed into one another to produce a new visual image, or in metaphor, where the juxtaposition of words creates consonance in dissonance and enjoins the reader to perceive a new semantic pertinence. In the present context I mean by scumbling both a creative device and a critical perspective: it overextends the folds of one thing (fiction) into those of another (history) without eliminating entirely the discreteness of each. As a way of approximating history and fiction, scumbling deliberately opens truth and meaning to the contingencies of configuration and shows how discourse is used to tell a story whose essential and universal referent, as Ricoeur argues throughout his *Time and Narrative*, is time itself.[6]

It is clear that the intimacy of historical and fictional narration has been subvented in recent years by a common sense of its own, though this subvention has nurtured a relatively small body of writing. What "everybody knows" within this body (i.e., its enunciated normative values) is revealed by the nature of narration, which serves as the formative and communicative device of both history and fiction. In broad terms, narration is posited as a series of events (real or imagined) that have been configured by language to convey meaning. In both historical and fictional narration the author chooses what is relevant for inclusion in the desired configuration, as well as what elements are appropriately excluded, either because they are considered tangential to the material at hand or because their inclusion runs counter to the story as the narrator wishes to emplot it. In the case of history, as White points out, the narrative seems to convey a desire to have real events framed in coherence and integrity as a way for the reader to comprehend them fully (*Content* 1–25). Furthermore, it is precisely because historical events contain within them a narrative structure (i.e., life is sequenced in time) that historians are justified in using stories as legitimate representations of events and, therefore, in viewing these representations as valid explanations of historical realities. In fiction the same qualities of completeness and congruity may be perceived as intensifying the referential base of the work (i.e., the story of human experience is reflected by the story of literature) or, conversely, as ingenuous and inappropriate. This is especially the case in the twentieth century, when fiction often consciously eschews straightforward narration in favor of a more peripatetic one. In either case, however, the configuration of events turns upon the notion of referentiality: the perception that one narrative strategy or the other more accurately illustrates life as we are able to know and give meaning to it. In large part, therefore, preoccupation with mimetic adequacy motivates both forms of narrative strategy. As Ricoeur astutely notes, "The argument for verisimilitude has merely been displaced. Formerly, it was social complexity that called for abandoning the classical paradigm; today, it is the presumed incoherence of reality that requires abandoning every paradigm" (*Time* 2: 14). Integrity and closure in historiography or in traditional Realistic fiction seek to convey what is essential and reveal the deep meaning of the events narrated, and a like argument can be made for the openness and opacity of contemporary fictional narratives. The paradigm of incompleteness in fictional discourse is found in the world (i.e., the narrative paradigm is mimetically adequate to life), hence the revealed meaning stems from the perceived coincidence between reality and narrative form.

Above all, historical and fictional narratives share the configurational element of temporality. Both fiction and history are symbolic discourses to the extent that they mediate human perception of the workings of life. Furthermore, both configure their narratives in order to draw out what is pertinent and revealing about existence. What emerges as most pertinent, and what is ultimately revealed by each, are the aporias of human time. As White notes, speaking of Ricoeur, "If histories resemble novels this may be because both are speaking . . . 'symbolically' about the ultimate referent [time]" (*Content* 175). The issue of time in historiography is crucial for Ricoeur because he insists that historical narrative imitates human actions, which are driven through time by the overt intention to achieve meaning. Ricoeur argues that human lives aspire to coherence (meaning), which allows the historian to discern the beginnings, middles, and ends inherent in human actions. Husserl's assertion that time is "the form of experience" is highly pertinent here, since it is through narration that this experience is symbolically revealed. Historical discourse follows a pattern originally laid out by events, but these events *coupled* with narration are what give to historiography epistemological thickness.

The consequences of Ricoeur's position are extreme, of course, because they preclude a historiography modeled on experimental and antinarrativist discourse. Historiography rejects this kind of writing, primarily because it refuses to submit to the authority of coherence and integrity that Ricoeur finds in the intentionality of all human actions. Certainly, it is not the case that the historian thinks less complex thoughts than the novelist, or that history itself is perceived as exempt from the enigmatic. It is rather that the historian will admit ambiguity and indeterminacy only at the level of content (i.e., all of the facts are not known), as if form were a matter apart, a container that holds the more important material of what the story is about. Hayden White is less restrictive in this regard, but he views the problem only from the side of history. He asserts that the plots of history may depend as forcefully upon the strategies of narration as upon the "found" plots within events themselves, but he does not resolve the more complicated issue of the commingling of historical and fictional purposes in a single work.

The positions of both White and Ricoeur may be broadened, however, with postmodern conceptions of narration, in which traditional generic boundaries grow ambiguous and the human experience of time and its structures is drawn forth in a variety of narrative paradigms. Within the postmodern conception, linguistic texts are constructed with no felt need to conform to perceived laws from the world outside the text. Thus what might be called the "meaning" of a text, which traditionally has depended to at least some degree on representational "accuracy," is now shaped and reshaped through the play of signifiers incapable of drawing into our presence anything but the designs of their own composition. Since the link between language and reality is fragile to begin with, and since whatever really did happen in the past is now placed within a narrative system that can only confirm the absence of the real, then we are left to ponder history plagued by chaos and distress. The primacy of narration supplants the primacy of the mind (conjoined with the world) in the constitution of meaning, which in turn compels history and fiction to collapse into amorphous and unpredictable relationships defined by varying perceptions of writers and readers.

For New Historicists, such as Stephen Greenblatt, this means that literary and historical texts circulate inseparably within culture and therefore traverse various interpretive communities. Since no discourse is able to (re)present unchanging truths and inalterable meanings, the crucial task for historians and literary critics alike is to adopt (or create) a discourse that enjoins the confluence of traditional esthetic and historical spheres. As Greenblatt argues, critical formulations for understanding history and literature must "[pull] away from a stable, mimetic theory of art . . . and construct in its stead an interpretive model that will more adequately account for the unsettling circulation of materials and discourses that is . . . the heart of modern aesthetic practice" (12–13). Within this scheme, all knowledge of the past is perceived as contingent and discontinuous. It is of course uninterpretable *once and for all,* but remains always interpretable.

My purpose in the above discussion has not been to enter fully into the debate about sameness and difference in fiction and history, but rather to adumbrate the parameters of its principal ideas as they relate to the present study. I am in fact prepared to embrace the middle ground and celebrate the "common sense" offered by a diversity of positions. I am not proposing, however, a drift toward a bland critical center. My concern is to link history and fiction by exploring specific historiographic and fictional texts drawn from a particular period of time—post–Civil War Spain. The question to be addressed here, therefore, is not whether history and fiction are bound up by shared intentions, references, and the engendering devices of narration in a general way (they clearly *are* and *are not*), but rather what implications arise for meaning and for truth from the juxtaposition of texts from Francoist historiography and postwar Spanish fiction, which have both history and the writing of history as referent.

With few exceptions, the critical study of these matters in Francoist Spain has been largely neglected. It is not that scholars have failed to explore various challenges to authority represented by fiction in general (or by literature as a whole) in postwar Spain—traditional historical methodologies have long pushed Hispanic studies in this direction. Rather it is that the idea of history, when addressed at all, has generally been viewed as a question of content, with the concomitant interest in accuracy of representation. As a result, our critical procedures have generally resisted making history itself problematic. This has certainly been the case, for example, in the important overviews of the postwar novel written during the 1970s and 1980s (Gonzalo Sobejano's *Novela española de nuestro tiempo,* Santos Sanz Villanueva's *Tendencias de la novela española actual,* Ignacio Soldevila Durante's *La novela desde 1936,* and others like them), which generally provide brief biographical sketches, lists of important novels, classifications of narrative tendencies, and commentaries on selected works. Although these studies refrain from proposing a master discourse that integrates key images, facts, and meanings of literary history, their critical procedures do not advance the futility of such an undertaking. Rather, they imply its possibility.

Even in those studies that have pursued history (and the broader category of "culture") as the center of their project, history generally retains the standing of a truth (or lie) to be discovered rather than a meaning to be constructed. History thus becomes a horizon against which literary texts come fully into focus while also providing stability for the pursuit of a unitary meaning. A few examples from recent critical work on postwar literature will elucidate the point. In her book *Rojos y rebeldes* Shirley Mangini points to the historical value of social realistic novels, but primarily underscores the accuracy of their representations. In other words, such novels become documents to be used by historians either seeking to set straight the facts of life under Franco or attempting to identify specific historical tendencies. Mangini implies in her study that the materials of history are internally organized systems, coherent and complete, that already bear a given meaning. The writer's task in recording them, therefore, confers a fixed authenticity to their standing in the world.

Abigail Lee Six ventures beyond the representational and draws forth historiography in her study of Juan Goytisolo ("Breaking Rules, Making History"), but she comments principally on Goytisolo's practice of mixing past and present "content" in his fiction as a way of violating historical method. Such an approach constrains her to make the traditional fact/fiction distinction in a general way, but more importantly, it compels her to a theoretical divergence: she calls forth postmodern thinking in her study of fiction (which examines not life but language) and at the same time advances the traditional material of history when defining historiography—"the recording of real life in the past" (42). Jo Labanyi, in her intelligent and important study of the postwar novel (*Myth and History in the Contemporary Spanish Novel*), moves to the outer edge of historiography in order to reveal how certain novels of postwar Spain ironically subvert Francoist assumptions that history reproduces universal relations. Labanyi intervenes in the fact/fiction dichotomy through her placement of historical and fictive narratives in the neutralizing domain of myth. Yet as she squeezes history into the confining parameters of myth, she does so (in contrast to her study of fiction) without scrutinizing the writing of history at close range.

It is clear that a willingness to explore historical circumstance underpins much critical work on the postwar Spanish novel. Indeed, the studies mentioned above (as well as others like them) have helped to uncover the symbolic management of history that impinges upon much postwar writing and have defined the circumstances in which this writing was produced. Barry Jordan's *Writing and Politics in Franco's Spain*, for example, is sharply cognizant of historical context in the development of social realism in the 1950s, as is Pablo Gil Casado's *La novela social española* or Fernando Morán's *Novela y semidesarrollo*.[7] The performative tenets of these studies, however, generally grow from the assumption that the novel offers up a set of problems whose shape is more or less stable and whose understanding depends upon a set of critical practices that are more or less adequate to the task at a given moment. But the premise might also be stated conversely: the novel is constituted by the field of questions that we pose and the historically variable value judgments that we make. If history-as-content is relocated in our studies within the larger discursive field of historiography, the questions that correlate with this placement necessarily alter both the focus of critical inquiry and the meanings that are advanced. In other words, we are compelled to abandon the ingenuous assumption that history speaks for itself and that the meaning (and truth) of the past emerges apodictically.

The crucial task at hand, therefore, is to avoid the hegemony over the past granted to the mimetic adequacy of fiction and history, and to draw to the fore the potential locations where their discourses intersect and reshape the past. For this reason the nature of historiography under the Franco regime is crucial to my project, and in chapter 1 I lay out the principal norms that underpin the writing of history in Spain during the first two decades following the Civil War. The pattern of discourse offered by historians of the State enabled them to create and sustain a coercive power over ideas about the past, with the dual aim of stifling dissent and controlling the sense of history. I am particularly concerned in this chapter with the rhetorical and narrative principles espoused by historians of the Regime, as well as the Catholic / Falangist perspective that shapes and defines the Francoist understanding of the past.

The fictive texts that stand opposed to the historiographic texts of the Regime are by no means bound up by a narrow set of literary principles: they speak with a broad range of voices and are constructed with variable amounts of traditional, experimental, and antinarrativist techniques. In chapter 2, I examine the way in which perhaps the most traditional form of writing in postwar Spain, the social realistic fiction of the 1950s, contests the mythic foundations of Francoist historiography. Although at first glance social realism seems to stand only as a homology of the real in *present* time, this "realness" serves to echo an implied past that explicitly challenges history as it is propagated by the State. Through paradox and irony, social realistic novelists subvert the mythic and heroic ordering of history offered up by historians of the Regime. But they do so in large part through the creation of countermyths rather than through the sublation of the process within which the past is controlled and made known by Francoist historiography. In contrast, the novel of memory, which I discuss in chapter 3, works consistently to decenter the paradigms of mythic discourse used by the State. In the novel of memory, the historical past of Spain is explored as time filtered through the consciousness of a self at once in history (the present) and open to the multiple meanings of history made available through the necessary process of interpretation. In other words, the center of historical inquiry becomes a movable construct that is always framed by an individual whose subjectivity determines the contingency of historical meanings and whose dissent is born from the hermeneutics of memory and narration.

In chapter 4 I turn to the writings of Juan Benet, the postwar novelist who focuses his work most compellingly on the relationship between history and fiction. Benet's theoretical writings, his own historiography, as well as his novels, address the parameters of reference and self-reference in a way that forges a unique narrative intimacy between history and fiction. His novels show how discursive configuration co-exists with what is often perceived as "fact" in highly referential narration, and he points to the way in which the tellers of a story—a story of history or of fiction—project both themselves and the reader imaginatively into history in order to understand beyond the surface level of event.

It is important to point out, however, that Benet's pivotal admixture of word and world, knowledge and interpretation, and the meanings conferred upon the past, is not the last word on the matter in postwar Spain. Within the same temporal context, and largely in contrast to both Benet and other novelists discussed here, the concern with history and historiography informs a broad range of postmodern fictions in Spain during the late 1960s through the early 1980s. As I show in chapter 5, Camilo José Cela's *San Camilo, 1936* and certain narrations of Gonzalo Torrente Ballester and Juan Goytisolo assert the end of historiography. They do so by privileging the power of words as the primary foundation of power within an aleatory narrative of deferral. This leads to the conclusion, in chapter 6, that the collapse of narration in the postmodern novel folds into the triumph of pure fiction. The radical discontinuities between narrations, representations, and meanings are both apocalyptic and revolutionary in postmodern novels, whose project is to disavow textual meanings that are an effect of reference to the world, and therefore, to history. As I suggest, however, the postmodern premise is apocalyptic not only in its desire to put an end to history (past time *in reality*), but more importantly, it is apocalyptic in its root capacity to reveal and transform. Although the triumph of fiction in postmodern texts sets out (as Ihab Hassan has noted in another context) to dismember Orpheus, in the end this triumph gives rise to narrative possibilities that not only open narration to new and complex paradigms, but also open the world (through the text) to new and complex meanings.

The salient issue at hand, therefore, is not what empirically real objects are represented by the fiction and history of postwar Spain (I am not concerned, for example, with what may or may not have happened in the bombing of Guernica during the war), but rather from which textualizations do the works of history and fiction most fully reveal their capacity to mean. In each set of texts that I study the past assumes a form, a vocabulary, and a meaning within a normative set of strategies that make it available to us. My purpose is to disclose these strategies in historiography and fiction, as well as the *conception* of narrating history that the strategies convey, in order to reveal the imbrications of truth and meaning that lie at the heart of much narration about the past in Spain from the early 1940s to the demise of Francoism.

I

Co-opting the Past:

Historiography in Francoist Spain

It is not possible to exterminate the conquered.

—Manuel Tuñón de Lara,

"Pórtico: Primero de abril de 1939"

In 1958 Manuel Fraga Iribarne (then director of the Instituto de Estudios Políticos) published an article in *Arbor* on the recently promulgated "Ley Fundamental de 17 de mayo." The new law did little to alter the legal or political standing of Spanish government under Franco. It reaffirmed the founding principles of the Regime, which had been approved by national referendum in 1947, and it certified the moral and historical legitimacy of Franco's rule as "Jefe del Estado" ("Chief of State"). But in his article Fraga sought to expand the implications of the new law by attaching to it a sweeping reprobation of dissent. Not only were the laws of the State "permanent and unalterable," but they constituted the normative values of Spain "before God and before History" (516). Most importantly, however, Fraga concluded that, "All that stands outside of the Principles [of the National Movement] is revolution" (517).

Fraga's declaration of conformity and consonance offers in brief the broad doctrine of coerced acquiescence, which shaped the intellectual posture of the Regime during much of Franco's rule.[1] The weight of coercion is especially pertinent to the writing of history, since it created and sustained what the historian Henry Steele Commager describes as necessary to the sustenance of any political state: a usable past. For the Franco regime, this means that the State used the past both to underpin its existence as the fulfillment of Spain's historical destiny and to give moral legitimacy to its claim of authority in the present. As Franco pursued historical justification for his regime, he adopted a strategy that turned upon a conservative and counterrevolutionary view of history during the 1940s and 1950s that was sustained by key institutions of the State: the Ministry of Information and Tourism (censorship); universities and academic disciplines (even under the moderately liberal Joaquín Ruiz Giménez, Minister of Education from 1951 to 1956); intellectual journals and magazines; and research bodies such as the Consejo Superior de Investigaciones Científicas.[2] The publication of Julio Caro Baroja's *Los judíos en la España moderna*, submitted for approval to the Ministry of Information and Tourism in 1960, offers a pertinent example of how the government held a firm hand on the affairs of the past through censorship. Several segments of the work, from criticism of the Inquisition to the assertion that religious unity in Spain during the sixteenth and seventeenth centuries was constantly undermined by "crypto-freethinkers," were suppressed or rewritten in order to appease government objections. As Manuel Abellán rightfully observes, the censorship of the Caro Baroja book "[illustrates] the untouchability of Spanish historiography as it was conceived by Francoism through censorship" (180).

But censorship represents only a small part of the Regime's authority over history. Indeed, while it is compelling for what it disallows about the meaning of Spanish history, censorship is secondary to the Francoist posture defined by what the State actually affirms and controls through its own historical discourse. To a large degree, Francoist historiography does not aim to dispute the knowledge collectively possessed about the past of Spain (the so-called facts of history), but rather seeks to establish a normative set of strategies that define a particular *concept* of history. The consequences of this intentionality are twofold: (1) Francoist historians assert and subsequently sustain their dominion over time and narration, so that history systematically emerges as myth; (2) historians of the Regime draw forth meaning in history that stands resolutely as the equal of truth, hence historiography assumes the secondary but no less important function of disallowing dissent. The conceptual presuppositions of Francoist historiography are highly prescriptive and serve to narrow the cognitive range within which the past can be properly understood. Historians of the Regime generally set out to cast historical "realities" into a narrative structure that negates alternative or counterdiscourses and therefore to make the past largely immune from other potential representations. The insistence by Francoist historiographers on sustaining "loyalty to the meaning of our history" (Pérez Embid, "Nueva actualidad" 153) asserts the centrality of a monological discourse through which the essential meaning of history remains always the same.

Claude Lévi-Strauss has wisely noted that "History is . . . never history, but history for" (257). Yet nearly the entire historiographic infrastructure of the State under Franco, whose actions in fact confirm Lévi-Strauss's maxim, assumed a theoretical posture advancing precisely the contrary. The intent became to convert what in reality was a cultural and political proposition about the past into what appeared to be a wholly natural *fact*. The most persistent strategy used to achieve this goal was to dress the principle of "truth by assertion," which shaped the tautological fabric of Francoist historiography (i.e., the past is how we say it is because we say so) with the objectifying clothing of science. Thus, for example, the strong affiliation that existed between history and historiography in the 1940s and 1950s and the journal *Arbor*. Founded in 1943 by Rafael Calvo Serer, Raimundo Paniker, and Ramón Roquer, *Arbor* became an official publication of the Consejo Superior de Investigaciones Científicas in 1944.[3] As Gonzalo Pasamar Alzuria notes, "the Consejo was a lever of power for some professors ["catedráticos"] of History and catapult toward a professorship for others" (130). Although *Arbor* addressed (as did the Consejo) a wide range of intellectual topics throughout the 1940s and 1950s, it promptly set out to advance the views of the conservative Catholic faction of the Regime in matters related to history, and served to counter the mildly centrist posture of journals such as *Escorial* and *Revista de Estudios Políticos*.[4]

Even a cursory examination of *Arbor*, however, reveals that the surface cover of scientism suggested by its affiliation with the Consejo (and the concomitant principles of accuracy, truth, and objectivity) is undercut by the narrow ideological perspective embraced by its editors. In volume 1, for example, following a blessing and statement of endorsement by Pope Pius XII, the editors define the purpose of the journal: "*Arbor* . . . has proposed as a goal: to restore to Spanish thinking its profound and glorious meaning that is both traditional and Catholic: to urge Spanish science, since it is an aspiring toward God, to pursue truth and goodness with the unity of Christian philosophy" ("Prefacio" n.p.). Such thinking is of course fully consonant with the Consejo itself, which excluded liberal-minded historians from economic and academic programs while embracing historians "prepared to give cultural prestige to the Regime and to do everything possible to accommodate its requests" (Pasamar Alzuria 146).

Even after several years of publication, when political circumstances made it appear far less risky to loosen the intellectual hold on history, *Arbor* continued to affirm ideological rigidity in the formulation of Spain's past. For example, in an attack on Pedro Laín Entralgo's conception of "España como problema" in 1949, the managing editor of *Arbor*, Florentino Pérez Embid, reaffirmed the journal's original statement of intention. His essay not only strips bare the scientific camouflage of *Arbor*'s representation of Spanish history, but also exposes the core of its project to impose a unified and clear definition of Spain's mission: "The common mission of all of us is sufficiently clear, and is drawn with sufficient historical force, so that it informs a general attitude that is fruitful in itself. With this in mind, the possibility of a clearly defined and exemplary Spain, capable of pronouncing words that are valuable for all men, has shaped the work of those of us at *Arbor*. In service of this mission we insist upon intellectual precision and a firm resoluteness" ("Nueva actualidad" 157). The adumbration of "a clearly defined and exemplary Spain" overrides the impartial exploration that in theory shapes historical study. As a result, Spanish historiography overtly assumes a doctrinaire view that advances truth through the unifying tradition of Catholicism.

The broader issue of publishing in Spain also became immured in the intellectual suppositions of the Regime. For example, *Bibliografía General Española e Hispanoamericana*, official bibliographic tool of the State, assumed the responsibility of promoting the diverse aspects of publishing during the 1940s, but did so with narrow ideological pronouncements. In its first issue in 1941, following a five-year hiatus because of the war, the journal declares that it is now resuming the urgent task of invigorating the book industry. It does so, of course, with full awareness of its place and privilege within Francoist Spain: "The Official Book Councils of Spain would be greatly pleased if all of those who read [the Bibliography] would notice the differences of form and content in it, as in all things Spanish, that the National Crusade has prompted" (7). The larger working frame for its program, however, is shaped by an overt special pleading that elevates Franco to cultural (not merely military) icon:

> If supporting the providential man, who in the darkest hours of our History was able to become the inspired captain of twenty million men and twenty centuries of civilization and lead us to triumph, is a necessary act of patriotic gratitude, even more so is the case when *Bibliografía* gives gratitude in the name of the savior of a marvelous culture that, had his inspired hand trembled, would have been in danger of fatally perishing.
>
> *Bibliografía* . . . repeats with emotion in its first issue, which appears on the second anniversary of the Victory, the name of the Caudillo: Franco! Franco! Franco! Viva España! Arriba España. (9)

During the 1940s, Francoist historiographers continued to extol professional rigor in the writing of history, despite the ideological rigidity that regularly shaped their ideas. In the fall of 1942, for example, at the convocation ceremonies in Madrid at the Universidad Central, the historian Manuel García Morente gave a lecture titled "Idea para una filosofía de la Historia de España." A decade before, García Morente had been denounced by the political Right for his impassioned defense of the Republic. Following the war, however, his newly minted conservatism asserted a firm renunciation of historiography that did not account for "intuition" (i.e., conservative ideology) as a necessary creative component of historical writing and that excluded nationalist and Catholic hegemony over the past. Such thinking was generally reflective of the whole of Francoist historiography and underscored in particular the strong antiliberal posture adopted by historians throughout the 1940s and 1950s. José Antonio Primo de Rivera's famous declaration that Spain's essence lay in the "unity of destiny in the universal" was often cited by these new historians of the Regime in order to distinguish Spain's authentic past from the liberal interpretations of nationalism during the nineteenth and early twentieth centuries. The historiographic enterprise thus became an overt political act bound up with the Catholic / Falangist conception of truth. As Alonso del Real wrote (paraphrased by Pasamar Alzuria), the purpose was to "demand from the historian a militant commitment that assumed 'preconceived ideas' . . . which embodied values defined by their opposition to those of the nineteenth century ('positivism,' 'liberalism,' etc.)" (Pasamar Alzuria 191).

The antiliberal perspective remains crucial to historians of the Regime throughout the postwar years and eventually becomes a way not only to understand (and lament) the independence movements of Spain's colonies in America during the nineteenth century, but also to adumbrate the larger issue of the collapse of Spanish imperialism. As Vicente Palacio Atard (Professor of Modern History at the University of Valladolid) noted in 1949, the traditional explanations of Spanish decay by liberal historiography (e.g., religious intolerance, expulsion of the *moriscos,* an Austrian monarchy that never understood the Spanish soul, lack of *"civismo"* among the Spanish) failed to get to the root cause of the matter. The genuine explanation for Palacio Atard was simple and direct, and turned upon the persistent diminution (until the Franco regime) of Catholic ideals. As he succinctly puts it, "in Spain, men did not fail, ideas did" (*Derrota* 165).

It was also during this period that Marcelino Menéndez y Pelayo emerged as one of the principal sources of historiographic guidance among Francoist historians. *Arbor* devoted a special issue to the Spanish thinker in 1956 to honor the centenary of his birth, and its editors offered a concerted plan to enthrone him as the paragon of scientific historians. Palacio Atard, for example, noted that Menéndez y Pelayo "bequeathed us, above all, an invaluable model as a man of science and historian of Spain" ("Menéndez y Pelayo" 429), and later added, "Because Menéndez y Pelayo was an authentic man of science, there coexists in him a suspicious fear of historical synthesis and a powerful gift for synthesis, which all of us recognize as the most distinctive quality of this great historian of Spain" (432).

But Menéndez y Pelayo had assumed a critical position in Francoist historiography long before the special issue of *Arbor* in 1956. In 1946, for example, Rafael Calvo Serer celebrated the wisdom of Menéndez y Pelayo's historical vision: "Since the young generation completely rejects revolutionary abstractions, loyalty to national destiny leads the Spain of today to its great historian, Menéndez y Pelayo" ("Nueva generación" 235). Two years later, Pérez Embid reaffirmed Menéndez y Pelayo's centrality to Francoist historiography with a tribute to him in *Arbor:*

> *Arbor* has proclaimed this very year its fundamental loyalty to Menéndez y Pelayo's conception of Spain. . . . Don Marcelino . . . represents for us a permanent conception of Spanish existence. . . . And we—Spaniards who are aware of the tenuousness of nationalisms in conflict—, in order to seek a superior unity in the field of culture, begin with the conception of Spain that don Marcelino constructed with the definitive materials of his time. . . . Faced with the ruin offered by the principles of modernity and by its Spanish imitations, we seek—facing the entire Hispanic world—the historic vitality of that marvelous plan of Spain that don Marcelino formulated. ("Nueva Actualidad" 153)

Pérez Embid not only integrates here Menéndez y Pelayo's ideas fully within the historiographic canon of the Regime, but sanctifies his position by using the semantic topoi of fascist rhetoric. Expressions such as "permanent conception of Spanish existence," "superior unity," or "historical vitality" are clearly intended to co-opt for the Regime the writings of an intellectual icon. As Pasamar Alzuria astutely has written: "The achievement of the *Arbor* group was to transform [Menéndez y Pelayo] into a lay-Catholic Francoist *avant la lettre*" (116).

For Menéndez y Pelayo the past and future of Spain both begin and end with Catholic religiosity and orthodoxy. He repeatedly challenges the perception of history formulated by the free-thinking Krausists of the Institución Libre de Enseñanza (he accuses them of disaffirming the religious essence of the Spanish past), but more importantly, he places at the intellectual center of his work the idea of an authentic and eternal Spain.[5] As Palacio Atard notes, Menéndez y Pelayo embraced "the unquestionable conviction that the nation is not a historic, temporal, and contingent entity in the whole of its purity, but rather it [the nation] is rooted in an atemporal principle of permanence" ("Menéndez y Pelayo" 434–44). On the one hand, Menéndez y Pelayo's insistence upon the permanence of Spanish history is highly ironic, since atemporality, which is used to shape a supremely temporal endeavor, would seem to compel the erasure of history as a vital force for change and progress. In fact, as I will suggest throughout this study, the historiographic posture of the Regime does indeed serve to diminish history and nullify its vast potential to bear a diversity of meanings. On the other hand, however, the concept of atemporality is an especially powerful enticement for historians of the State, and its value as a historiographic concept can be discerned in two important branches of their thinking.

The first stems from the importance attached to the study of history as an integral component of the Regime's program to shape the present and future time of Spain. Menéndez y Pelayo was not a political figure by profession (he was an unsuccessful candidate for Parliament in 1884), but his ideas were co-opted by Francoist historiographers for specifically political ends. For example, in 1949, in his response in *Arbor* to Laín Entralgo's mildly dissident *España como problema*, Calvo Serer insists upon the crucial impingement of the Spanish past upon the constitutive elements of Francoist Spain. He quotes Menéndez y Pelayo's *Ensayos de crítica filosófica* to buttress his position: "A people that does not know its history is a people condemned irrevocably to death: it may produce brilliant, isolated individualities, flashes of passion, of creativity and even of genius, and these will be like lightning bolts that accentuate the darkness of the night" ("Sin problema" 165).

More significantly, however, Calvo Serer had appropriated Menéndez y Pelayo's thinking two years earlier (without attribution), but with a decisive twist that infuses the entire historiographic enterprise of Franco with conceptual insularity. Calvo Serer wrote in 1947 that "a people that does not know the meaning of its history is condemned to irremediable death, given that their efforts can only be positive and fertile if they follow the path of national tradition; loyalty to one's own history is a necessary condition for a creative culture" ("Nueva generación" 334). While Calvo Serer draws upon Menéndez y Pelayo to structure a particular perception of history that slices away all impurities from discourse on the past ("loyalty to one's own history") and co-opts his aphorism on the value of knowing the past, he introduces a critical semantic change. By adding the word "meaning"—the meaning of history—to Menéndez y Pelayo's valuation of the past, Calvo Serer edges closer to a fuller grasp of the writerly component of history. But there is both a truism and a paradox in his position. On the one hand, it is no longer merely a question of knowing the past. Indeed, history is not the past as such, but the force that sweeps the past into the present. This force takes root in the authority of narration and thus moves the strategies of historiographic composition to the fore. Furthermore, this new emphasis on writing suggests the full range of aporias inherent in all discourses that seek to represent the real. But the paradox of Calvo Serer's position surfaces in his refusal to allow the process of writing to give a meaning to history not already inscribed in the tradition of orthodoxy. In other words, he opens history to the contingent nature of meaning, but since his project is to sanctify what is permanent and essential, he closes off history from the very provisionality that his historiographic posture implies.

When Calvo Serer urges that "one cannot vacillate in rejecting those elements that make themselves unassimilable into the national and orthodox unifying tradition. The only synthesis possible is one made upon the foundation of the most loyal orthodoxy" ("Del 98" 29), or when Pérez Embid affirms that diversity in evoking the past threatens "the permanent meaning of [Spanish] history" ("Nueva actualidad" 149), the historiographic agenda of the government crystallizes in the consequences of its discourse: the rule of Franco has a firm hold not only on history as event (the "facts" of the past), but also on the meaning of that history as discourse. Francoist historiographers reject narrations that undermine conformity as the cohort of truth, hence what remains is the comfort of certainties buttressed feebly by the absence of dissent. As Randolph Pope has shown about the writing of history during this period, "[Historiography] seeks out *one* point rather than many, since the concept of unity is central, advanced by the philological and Castilianist historical school which reduces the history of Spain to that of Castile" ("Historia y novela en la posguerra española" 17). Polyphony thus becomes the fatal casualty of Francoist historiography. The meaning of the past is squeezed into the safe zone of orthodoxy, unity, and narration as defined by Menéndez y Pelayo and subsequently dispersed by historians of the Regime.

Pope's brief reference to Castile is an important one, since the concept of Castile as the vital embodiment of Spain and its values informs much of Francoist historiography. Historians of the Regime not only link Castile to the birth of Spain as a nation during the reign of Isabel and Ferdinand, but equally significant, relate the region to the Reconquest and myth of unification under Catholicism and to the spiritual foundations of Spanish imperialism and conquest. In 1944, for example, Francoist historians celebrated the millennium of the birth of Castile with a series of new scholarly studies as well as the reinterpretation of old ideas.[6] While Spanish historians had long studied the Middle Ages and had offered valuable insights into its role in Spanish history (e.g., the work of Menéndez Pidal and Sánchez Albornoz), historians of the Regime sought to squeeze the permanent values of this authentic and original Spain into the narrow frame of Falangist/Catholic hegemony. Menéndez Pidal (and before him, Menéndez y Pelayo) had already drawn forth the conservative Catholic perspective on the Castilian Middle Ages when he argued in 1934 for the "national imperialist concept" ("De la vida" 155) that had been inherited from Castile. But more importantly, Francoist historians allied the Castilian character of Spain with the persistent kindling of the heroic in Spanish history, which in turn was embodied in contemporary Spain by the Francoist state and wrapped in the heavily partisan rhetoric of the Regime.[7] As Pasamar Alzuria notes:

> What before the Civil War had been one of the most solid contributions of constitutional history, the studies of Sánchez Albornoz on Medieval Castile, was presented in terms of the history of saints and heroes. What in Menéndez Pidal was a terminology borrowed from conservative essayists or from their analyses of the epic, in Brother Justo [Pérez Urbel] was an authentic reportoire of expressions from Falangist vocabulary: thus, Castile "was able to foresee the unity of destiny," forge a "national social" order, "establish a goal of legal and moral values," where everything was "energy, strength, youth, etc." (314)

Both the conceptualization of Castile and its heroes as the core of Spanish history and the rhetorical devices used to construct and sustain such a view, give a permanence to the myth of Castile in Francoist historiography that stood firmly against dissidence and contingency throughout the 1940s and 1950s.

The second critical component of Menéndez y Pelayo's influence on Francoist historiography hinges upon the concept of universal history. Menéndez y Pelayo consistently ascribed to Spain a unique and permanent historical personality rooted in its spiritual rather than material past. Ironically, it is the uniqueness of this spiritual past (i.e., what makes Spain different) that compels the nation to envision its history both within a larger frame of chronological time and beyond the geographic bounds of the Iberian Peninsula. As Palacio Atard writes, referring to Menéndez y Pelayo's sense of history and nationalism, "Let us point out that the religion (of Spaniards) is specifically a nonnationalistic religion, directly opposed to all partisanship, [an idea] which was so nobly denied from the very beginning by the divine word of Christ and by the apostles of His doctrine, among whom Saint Paul stands out for the brilliance of his language" ("Menéndez y Pelayo" 437).

The originating impetus for a universal history can be traced at least to Augustine's *City of God*, but the concept gains more elaborate development in modern times in Vico's *Scienza nuova* (1725). In general terms, universal history posits that the past is an untold story whose events can be joined into a coherent whole following a design located in the events themselves. The original concept of universal history, as well as the concomitant idea of an intrinsic pattern of meaning, bore its authority from divine Providence—that is to say, events are perceived always within the scheme of God's vision. In the eighteenth century, however, the universal was secularized, leaving the idea of a story that is "there," in the world, waiting to be told. Louis Mink writes concerning universal history (quoting Kant), "We cannot make sense of history . . . unless it is possible to discover in it a single theme, a 'regular movement,' so that 'what seems complex and chaotic in the single individual [nation] may be seen from the standpoint of the human race as a whole to be a steady and progressive though slow evolution of its original endowment'" (190). For Menéndez y Pelayo, of course, the original endowment of the human race can be framed only by the concept of a Christian God and the permanent meaning of His word.

The positioning of Spain within a universal rather than nationalist history may at first glance appear odd. Given the consistency with which Franco sought to legitimate his historical role within the essential values of Spain and its birth as a nation, it would perhaps seem more compelling for the Regime to shape the Spanish past as a commingling of unique national traits—the way in which it embraced, for example, the centrality of Castile. But the idea of a universal history not only served to enhance Spanish nationalism, it also enabled the Regime to trumpet the moral superiority of the Spanish past and to enunciate what it perceived as the nation's historical destiny. To accomplish this, Francoist historiographers drew upon a radically eclectic view of universal history. They assumed divine guidance at the point of origin but also granted an implicit structure to narration centered within the events themselves. Thus universal history begins with Catholicity and ends with a monological discourse that bears upon the conceptualization of history as related to time, structure, narration, and myth.

Francoist historiography expands Menéndez y Pelayo's conception of a universal history through the recurrent juxtaposition of the Spanish past to the past of the whole of Europe. This is done by bodying forth Christianity as the formative substance of history. Federico García Sanchiz's declaration in 1945 epitomizes Francoist rhetoric:

> Spain is the only country in History where there cannot be, nor has there been, nor is there any difference between moral and religious character and national historical character; because in Spain the Hispanic and the Christian are united, and they come to form a consubstantial whole. . . . One cannot be Spanish and not be Catholic, because if one is not Catholic, one cannot be Spanish. Whoever says that he is Spanish and not Catholic does not know what he is saying. . . . In Spain all men are gentlemen and Christians. (Rodríguez Puértolas 2: 993–94)

Although García Sanchiz's posture offers either conformity to Catholicity or exclusion from Spanishness, and appears to whip the rhetoric of Christian rule into an intransigent frenzy, his ideas stand close to the mainstream of historiographic thinking as set forth by historians of the Regime.

Perhaps less strident an influence during this time, but no less cogent in his intellectual reach, was the Russian philosopher Nicholas Berdyaev. Along with Spengler, who was earlier introduced to Spanish thinkers through *Revista de Occidente,* Berdyaev was widely read in Spain in the 1940s. Several of his works were translated into Spanish and excerpts from his writings appeared in journals throughout the decade.[8] Of particular importance is his *El sentido de la Historia,* published in Spain in 1943, which turns upon the author's concern with eschatology and suggests the historiographic tenet of exploring the past through the paradigm of exceptional periods. Most pertinent for historians of the Regime, Berdyaev asserts that the determinate periods of history are those in which the historical time of humanity and the divine time of God reach coincident fruition through the principles of Christ's incarnation. Berdyaev's conception of time and history argues that this full fruition was last attained during the Middle Ages when "Christianity alone had been the light and the principle of order" (*End* 102–03). He suggests that a "New" Middle Ages would reestablish the moral exigency of divine time and transform the present into an exceptional period of history. Similar to García Morente's emphasis on an intuitive (i.e., ideological) writing of history, Berdyaev's insistence on framing the past with Catholicity undermines the liberal positivism of turn-of-the-century historiography and advances in its place a reactionary paradigm of tradition and faith.

Such a view of course buttressed the position of historians of the Regime and their universalist intentions. While other countries in medieval times developed parochial and nationalistic tendencies, Spain, they argued, nurtured universalist ideas during eight centuries of fighting to protect Christianity. As the chosen nation of God (Manuel García Morente prefers the phrase "people especially called upon by God" [Rodríguez Puértolas 2: 992]), Spain eventually shaped the political and cultural landscape of Europe and fulfilled, as Primo de Rivera insisted a decade before the Franco government, its "unity of destiny in the universal." That is to say, for Francoist historiography the history of humankind reaches beyond the geographic borders of Spain as it is conceived as a nation in 1492, but Spain offers a unique embodiment of universal history centered on the idea of a permanent and essential set of spiritual values.

The first serious challenge to Spanish values (and to its preeminence in history) emerges in the Reformation, which is viewed by Francoist historians as a tragic disruption of the given plot of history and the end of an exceptional period of Christian incarnation. The disorder caused by the Reformation is not set straight, however, despite Spain's heroic attempts—this is the essence of Spanish imperialism—and soon engenders the spiraling fall toward secularization, liberalism, and the perversion of the universal Christian story during modern times. As Calvo Serer writes:

> The West, following the internal rupture and conflicts of the sixteenth and seventeenth centuries, replaced the unifying medieval and Christian culture with the open heterodoxy of the Enlightenment. At that time the incompatibility of Spain with the development of European history obligates it [Spain] to isolate itself from Europe, thereby intensifying its own political, cultural, religious, and social decay. In this way, what has been called Spanish decadence is more accurately understood as a fundamental discrepancy with modern Europe. ("Nueva generación" 339)

It must be pointed out, however, that Francoist historians did not seek to diminish in their scholarly writings the severity of Spanish decay in the post-Reformation world. In 1949, for example, Vicente Palacio Atard published *Derrota, agotamiento y decadencia en la España del siglo XVII,* while the problems associated with the political and economic decline of Spain for over two centuries were scrutinized frequently in the pages of *Arbor* during this period. In a curious way, Francoist historiographers even celebrated the decadence of Spain as the inevitable consequence of their nation's heroic resistance to the modern world. The nobility of this resistance could come fully into view only in the context of Francoist Spain, of course, when the normative principles of historiography hinged upon "loyalty to one's own history" and the allied concept of Spain's universal mission. Palacio Atard writes in his book, for example, "We have been accused of anti-Europeanism, we who have destroyed ourselves and have bled ourselves dry for Europe. We who have put our body and soul not only into Europe and America, but into the world. Yes, we live isolated from modern Europe, from what is lightly said to be Europe. Because Spain continues to be faithful to itself and because our unconditional values, today more esteemed than ever, are not in decay" (Sánchez Montes 617). When Calvo Serer contemplates the authentic and permanent history of Spain, he argues that to decry Spanish decadence is to betray the meaning and value of its history. The issue is not whether Spain lost its colonies and grew materially weak (it clearly did), but that it held firmly to the principles that gave it life as a nation to begin with. As Calvo Serer pointedly affirms concerning Spain's spiritual superiority, "Great undertakings are not measured by success—we were right and that is enough" ("Nueva generación" 342).

The shared perception among Francoist historiographers that "the history of Spain is universal history" (472) not only establishes the moral superiority of Spain in the broader story of human history, but also has important consequences for the unique body of historical traits forged by the Regime to define Spain as a nation. Since Francoist historiography begins by devising a single story for a universal history, the task then becomes one of positioning Spain within the same story. If the State envisages only one truth for a universal story of the Western World, so too does it offer one truth for the history of Spain. For those who propose a rhetoric of difference, or even for those who wish to defer closure concerning the past, the consequences of the State's position are harsh: both truth and meaning are collapsed into a single concept that steadfastly precludes dissent. As Palacio Atard writes, "Historical Spain, the Spain that the past has bequeathed us, is unique . . . and only when we discover its unique meaning will we cease to be led astray from the path of truth" ("Razón" 177). Although he does not evoke explicitly the concept of "Las dos Españas" here, Palacio Atard sanctions its importance through omission. Long countenanced by Spanish historiography as an abstract of liberal and conservative divisiveness in Spain since the Enlightenment, the idea of two Spains as a sound historiographic precept is quickly discarded by the Regime. When discussed at all, it is viewed as a perversion of true Spanish history in the context of the nation's universal mission. As Calvo Serer insists, "It is unthinkable to have more than one Spain: the one that sustains faithfully its universal mission, which began to be fulfilled in the sixteenth and seventeenth centuries. To the extent that we were unfaithful to that mission, Spain disappeared as a unity of destiny and returned to the tribalism of primitive peoples" ("Sin problema" 161).

The universal history propagated by the State excluded the concept of uniqueness and individuality (these were viewed as distortions motivated by ideological dissidents) and regarded differences as minor permutations of an immutable and essential Spain. The many potential permutations of the past bear scant importance; once identified, they are integrated into the underlying grid of a single Spain and traced upon the pattern of orthodoxy. This grid is of course the whole of Francoist historiography, and the orthodoxy, as we have seen, is configured largely by Menéndez y Pelayo. His claim that "Spanish genius is eminently Catholic: heterodoxy among us [is] an accident, a passing flash of light" (62) closely accommodates the intellectual program of the Regime, which declares with the self-endowed historical authority of its perceived mission, "We must maintain now at all costs the homogeneity achieved in 1939" (Calvo Serer, "Sin problema" 167).

But historians of the Regime set out not merely to expunge the concept of permutations from the authentic Spanish past. They also disaffirmed the notion of intellectual and political pluralism from which the concept had sprung. For example, in his highly regarded book, *El pensamiento de Cervantes*, Américo Castro criticizes Menéndez y Pelayo for writing from a conservative Catholic perspective. Although he praises Menéndez y Pelayo for occasionally offering "fine and exact observations" (14), he finds fault with much of what the Spanish thinker has proposed: "The vindication of Spanish science attempted by Menéndez y Pelayo was not always as effective as we would have wanted, due to its apologetic and superficial tone, and because it lacked a thoughtful comparison with current science in other countries; the political and religious prejudices of that great critic also served as an obstacle to the free pursuit of his research" (387–88).[9] But Calvo Serer, who was instrumental in enshrining Menéndez y Pelayo at the center of historiographic thought in the 1940s, not only contests Castro's historical perspective but also seeks to discredit it: "It is clearly a matter of imposing one's own convictions upon the past. Thus Castro's thesis, according to which Cervantes would be an astute dissembler of his own ideas, is merely a reflection of a more or less conscious desire to transform the spirit of Spanish history according to a specific ideology" ("Significación cultural" 320). What is implied here, of course, is wholly ironic: while Castro's position stems from a "specific ideology" and is therefore distorted, the affirmations of historians of the Regime are both objectively formulated and naturally correct.

A similar strategy was used by Pérez Embid in 1946 to asperse the publication of Angel del Río and M. J. Benardete's anthology of essays, *El concepto contemporáneo de España*. Pérez Embid attacks the book in a general way because it fails to embrace the canons of Francoist historiography, but two particular objections stand out: (1) the work ignores the writings of Menéndez y Pelayo and his followers ("No one less than Menéndez y Pelayo is left out of the anthology" ["Review" 490]), and (2) it excludes the ideas of Spanish intellectuals from the conservative publications *Acción Española* and *Cruz y Raya*. The book therefore offers a perverted view of history that is "sectarian, ill-willed, and cleverly one-sided" (493). Put more directly, and viewed in the context of the discourse of the Regime, the refusal by the authors of *El concepto contemporáneo de España* to conform to the historiographic canons of unity and orthodoxy taints their discourse and undermines the truth of their assertions.

The above two examples underscore how dissident historiography strained against the discourse of the Regime during the 1940s and 1950s, but was unable to gain independent standing. It is true that as early as 1951 Jaime Vicens Vives published the first issue of *Estudios de historia moderna*, in which he advocated a more objective approach to the writing of history, and Enrique Tierno Galván, in *XII tesis sobre funcionalismo europeo* (1955), urged the Regime to rid the academy of the "ideological absolutism" that contaminates the pursuit of truth (Díaz 142). Vicens Vives was especially important during this period because he pursued historical study within the frame of objectivity and scientism. He sought less to undermine the Regime than to locate objectivity at the root of historical study, and in general his writings follow the pattern of other dissident historians who, as Juan Marichal suggests, "find a way to fight against the essentialist rhetoric through very precise and erudite historiographic techniques" (Morán, *Explicación* 65). When laid beside the overtly ideological historiography of *Arbor*, for example, with its claims to scientific scrutiny, Vicens Vives's work reveals dramatically the special pleadings of the Regime and the distorted meaning that it attached to the past. But Vicens Vives did not have an easy time of it, despite his growing prominence in the academy during the 1950s. As Stanley Payne points out, Vicens Vives was forced to struggle "under the weight of a repressive state censorship and in an intellectual environment bound by rigid a priori schema" (120). These schema of course turned upon the Catholic suppositions of Menéndez y Pelayo and the essentialist reductivism of historians of the State. Thus despite the intentions of Vicens Vives and his followers, the overriding concern with historical hegemony remained firm during the two decades following the war, and historiography continued to prop up the myths on which the Franco regime had been constructed.[10]

The coupling of the past and future of Spain plainly coalesces in the historiography of the Regime through the insistent preoccupation with time. The very idea of writing history of course evokes past time. But historians of the State insinuate their discourse into the future as well, calling forth the importance of Spain's "historical destiny." The imposition of a historical destiny is critical to the functioning of Francoist historiography, and it stems from the pseudodeterministic principle that the essential Spain of the past (the truth of what has been) gives birth to the essential Spain of the future (the truth of what will be). The overextension of the past into the future creates scant risk for the Regime. Since the past is constituted fully by orthodoxy and consonance, its discourse and truth value both formulated and certified by the State, the "destino histórico" of Spain emerges as a natural filiation whose story needs simply to be told. Thus when Angel Ferrari writes that there is only one Spain, "that of its destiny in History" (108), or when Franco himself declares that "We are serving the destiny of Spain's historical greatness and we will continue to do so with more tenacity than that of the forces that try to block our path" (*Pequeño libro* 102), the aim of the Regime to control the past now expands to include control over the whole of time. It is in fact the interfusion of temporal divisions into a solidified oneness that the Regime pursues and eventually imposes.

Nicholas Berdyaev gave ample theoretical support to such a notion during this period. He argues in *The Meaning of History* that "[t]he only possible solution of universal history . . . is in terms of a victory over time, over its disruption into past, present, and future, over its disintegration into reciprocally hostile and devouring elements. The solution of the destiny of universal history involves the definitive conquest of time's corruptible nature" (190). For the understanding of Spanish history, this means that time is co-opted by the historiographic discourse of the State, whose project, as I have suggested, is to promote stasis (i.e., the future is equal to the past as defined by the State) and to dissociate meaning from the aporias of change. Since dissonance has been expurgated from history, the future-as-past assumes its natural place in the flow of time and thus bears the promise of continuity. As Palacio Atard affirms, synthesizing the historiographic posture of the Regime, "Our hope, when we begin to confront the current difficult times, as well as those that await us, is rooted in the strength of our past, in the fact that we have a rich past, a long history filled with meaning, and we will undoubtedly use an enormous dose of that past to shape the future" ("Actitud de revancha" 259). Palacio Atard's evocation of "a long past filled with meaning," coupled with the notion of "the strength of our past," not only reaffirms the awareness of the meaning attached to history, but in the full context of Francoist historiography defines that meaning within a narrow understanding of truth. José Antonio Biescas makes precisely this point in his recent history of the Francoist dictatorship: "the victors of '39 attempted to make a clean slate of all traditions that were not their own—dogmatic, institutionalized, identified with the nation; the rest was marginalized, expelled from intellectual acceptability" (Tuñón de Lara and Biescas 516). Both the past and future of Spain are thus shaped not through the concrescence of difference, but within a moral and ideological design that reflects a choice against the becoming of history in favor of a discourse of continuity.

Francoist historiography is resolutely shaped by a conception of truth and temporality in which history is viewed less as a complex web of diachronic and synchronic relationships, both formed and revealed through narration, than as an unfolding of time that is repetitive, deterministic, and radically unchangeable. Hence time (history) is perceived not as a progression or a becoming, but rather as a static entity anchored in all that is permanent and eternal. The kind of historiography that affirms these truths about the past, and the structures of narration embedded in its discourse, are rooted in the formative strategies of myth. The concept of myth is crucial to Francoist historiography, and I mean by it here the Barthean proposition that "the end of myth is to immobilize the world" (*Mythologies* 155). Myth in this context draws its power from the exaltation of sameness. It adheres to a pattern of discourse that eschews equivocation and ennobles all that is fixed and unvaried. As Frank Kermode has shown, myth propounds "a series of radically unchangeable gestures" (*Ending* 39). For historians of the Regime, this means that myth functions both to coerce belief and to compel silence in the laying out of the past, and its overriding power for the State stems from the intransigence of tautology: its truths are not a matter of confirmation but of affirmation; it turns not upon the intrusion of external facts but on the self-verifying immediacy of its own narrative structure.

The use of myth by historians of the State forcefully establishes the structure within which Spain must envisage its possibilities, while at the same time it proclaims a hierarchy of values and meanings within that structure. Perhaps most importantly, however, the assertions of myth preclude choice by making everything be as it must be. Myth denies that its discourse is made rather than found, and thus gives substance to the underlying assumption of universal history as conceived by the Regime. Myth forecloses upon the possibility of change by asserting the constancy of its truth on what it contends is the solid terrain of the real. More importantly, myth converts what at first are contingent assertions into a series of essences, which in turn imply their own necessity and certitude in the validating of truths about life. Like a parent responding to a child's persistent questioning, myth says forcefully that things are as they are because that's how they are (Barthes, *Mythologies* 153).

But Spanish historiographers do not perceive the reification of myth as the end point of their project. Hence they nudge historiography beyond myth and suggest that, in its intention and performance, the authentic history of Spain as a nation is postapocalyptic. Apocalypse of course bears the popular meaning of destruction and ruination, but more importantly, it suggests the end of transformation through the final epiphany of truth. Hence historians of the Regime aver that the present—the present of Franco—stands as a profound embodiment of postapocalyptic revelations of truth about the whole of the Spanish past. Such a view distends at once in several directions. It radically delimits the material of an authentic past as it is woven into the fabric of the present, and it defines the meaning of the past within a narrow frame of possibilities that perceives forms of dissonance as the ignoble debris of temporality. Franco himself articulated this perspective on a number of occasions. In October of 1948, for example, he declared, "In order for the History of Spain not to become distorted it is necessary for us to remain loyal to that spirit which illuminated the awakening of Spain—when scarcely were there nations in the world, when States had not been defined—whose laws and constitutions set an example for its own as well as other peoples" (*Franco* 96–97). That is to say, the postapocalyptic leveling of history, what Francoist historiography proclaimed as "the true Spain, the immortal Spain, the honorable Spain, the united Spain" (*Franco* 69) is validated through repetition and sustained by the eternalizing epic of the birth of Spain.

"The essential Spain" under the Franco regime, as well as its "historical destiny," therefore results from what Jo Labanyi has aptly described as the "fall into Paradise" (50), which in the present context is tied to the origins of Spain and nurtured by the postapocalyptic vision of stability and truth. The starting point for this vision, in chronological terms, is the expulsion of the infidels in 1492 and the subsequent divination of Isabel la Católica and the invention of Spain.[11] But 1492 represents not only the birth of Spain, it also stands as the apogee of Spain's moral and historical destiny. As Jesús Suevos argues in *Arbor* in 1958, "The super-nationalist historical destiny of Spain was revealed in a clear and extraordinarily precise way in the culminating moment of our history, when Spain, following its epic struggle of eight centuries, brings a happy and glorious end to the Reconquest" (325). The expulsion of the infidels is repeated in 1939, and the divination of Franco unfolds through the sacred circularity of myth. This idea is perhaps most explicitly conveyed in the historical biography of Franco published in 1939 by Fernando Herce Vales and Manuel Sanz Nogués. The work is titled *Franco, el Reconquistador* and is purely propagandistic, but it is of interest for the way it asserts in brief two formative principles of Francoist historiography: the filiation of Franco and the glorious acts of the Reconquest, and the assertion that these matters are absolutely true. As the authors write in the preface to their book, "Our desire is not to make a profit, which we do not want, because our activities have other goals. Rather [our desire] is to give all Spaniards a modest but honorable and historical meaning to the banner and supreme figure of the Caudillo with events from his life past and present, indisputable because they have come from reliable sources. Something very sincere, very truthful and eloquent. With the eloquence of truth" (4).

Franco himself, in one of his many speeches on the subject, also establishes the explicit link between past and present in the circle of time: "In the same way that the war of Liberation of Spain [the Civil War] was not an episode, but rather *the crowning of a historical process* . . . it is unacceptable to pass the sponge of forgetfulness over facts and events that are the foundation of our well-being and cause for so much sacrifice" (*Franco* 20, emphasis mine). This view of the Civil War as the "crowning of a historical process" enables Franco both to appropriate the past as the private enterprise of the State and to assert the permanent value of the present through the arresting of temporal progression. Following closely the ideas of Berdyaev here, Spanish historiographers suggest that history has positive significance only when attached to a culmination. As Berdyaev writes in *The Meaning of History*, "If history were an endless process, it would have no significance. The tragedy of time would admit of no resolution, the historical purpose of no realization, since neither the one nor the other can consist with historical time. The destiny of man implicit in the origins of history involves a super-historical goal, a super-historical consummation of history in eternal time" (205). This eternal time is deeply rooted in the universal history of Christianity (and of course in the authentic Spain), and reaches full fruition in the Middle Ages. Hence the Regime endeavors to stop time-as-progress and return to the age governed by Christian principle. Indeed, as Elías Díaz remarks concerning the temporal agenda of the Regime, "they seemed to see the Civil War as an instrument for attempting to stop or turn back time" (24).

The culmination of history that Franco proposes pulls the circle of consonance more tightly closed, and this tightness gains verbal sharpness in Franco's dictum "One Spain, one race, one religion." But the circle of consonance structures and limits the writing of history in such a way that it finally makes the past "unhistorical." By resorting to myth, Francoist historiographers imprison both time and discourse and thereby cut at the very heart of discovery and change that impel history to begin with. If as Mircea Eliade proclaims, "[m]odern man can be creative only insofar as he is historical" (156), and if Franco actually annuls the historical possibilities of "Man" by halting the progression

of time, then the tragic consequences of his historical perspective re-
sound with clarity: not only does the postapocalyptic "Paradise" pre-
side over the stability between past and present, it also gains full dominion over human creativity and potential that is projected toward the
future. In this sense Francoist historiography actually urges a radical
posthistory for Spain in which the struggle for liberation (the principal
impetus for historical change) is shown finally to have been won.[12]

The imposition of a posthistorical conception of time and history in
postwar Spain assumes that the battle for truth has already been waged,
that temporal progression has been stayed and re-formed as the consort
of stasis, and that the principal task of the future is the preservation of
the actual. In this sense, Francoist historiography vitiates the transcendence of historical knowledge by reducing it to one more political
instrument that plays harshly in the symphony of intellectual coercion.
Such coercion, as I have suggested, compels closure and sameness, and
the resultant fossilization of the past swindles history of its richness. As
Joseph Esposito writes, "If we assume that the study of history brings
saliently to focus the conditionality of human choices, then any society
in which that perspective is lacking is likely to become a blind society"
(135). In Francoist Spain, however, it is not that the historical perspective is lacking, but that the profusion of a single perspective anesthe-
tizes the past rather than awakens it to unfettered scrutiny.

In the end, however, Francoist historiography succeeds in suppress-
ing a discourse of dissent mainly within its own disciplinary ranks. Although it seeks to impose a univocal understanding of Spanish history
and to construct an institutional understructure hardened by myth, its
authority over time is dramatically fractured by a counterdiscourse
whose project disrupts, reshapes, and broadens the conception of the
Spanish past. This dissident conception celebrates the complicity between fiction and history and dramatizes the contingency of truth and
meaning inherent in all narration. The new perceptions that arise take
root in a body of fictional texts that contest the mythic discourse of the
State and offer alternative modes of writing about time and history.
The fiction to which I refer, and which is the focus of the remaining
chapters of this study, does not set out to explore the whole of Spanish
history in a form traditionally called the historical novel, providing an
alternative here or another perspective there on a particular event from

the Spanish past. Instead, it offers a diversity of discourses that speak to and against Francoist historiography, to and against the assumptions about time and history embraced by the State. Fictional texts perceived in the context of the historiography of the Regime thus become inoculations against darkness. In their most usable form, they are revealing perturbations that trigger dissent and dissonance, both in how the past is explored and the way in which it gains meaning in the present.

Social Realism and the Myths of

Historical Difference

If we write novels so, how shall we write history?
—Henry James, "George Eliot's *Middlemarch*"

One of the most intriguing forms of dissent within Spain from the history propagated by the State is shaped, somewhat paradoxically, by a group of novelists who published their first important works during the early 1950s—among others, Juan Goytisolo, Luis Goytisolo, Jesús Fernández Santos, Rafael Sánchez Ferlosio, and Carmen Martín Gaite. The paradox is not that dissent should spring from writers of "fictions," but that it inheres in a type of narrative (social realism) that focuses exclusively on present time. The paradox is easily set straight, however, if we pursue the larger field of intention (i.e., what the novelists intended to reveal and transform) and context (the implicit dialogue that social realism maintains with historical narration and temporal causality). Since the domain of the past had become the exclusive (and exclusionary) enterprise of the State under Franco, and since the truths set forth in that domain could not be directly contested through narration of the past, social realists set about depicting the full scope of the real in the present. Although the attachment of these novelists to history is perhaps less evident than that of writers who explore past time overtly, their dissent from the Regime's configuring of history is no less compelling in its reach and significance.

Social realism is a highly intentional mode of writing in postwar Spanish fiction. It emerged as a bounded but provocative form of narrative in the early 1950s, and came to a discernible close by the early years of the 1960s.[1] This brief chronological frame may be perceived as at once normative and generational: the tenets that defined social realism were both formulated and eschewed during a little more than a decade, and the novels produced were closely tied to writers bound up by common experiences of the Civil War and the intellectual antagonisms of postwar authoritarianism.[2] Over the course of a decade these novelists announced on several occasions what they sought to achieve in their works, and articulated as well a series of compelling strategies that gave shape to their novelistic discourse. Above all, they aspired to grasp life firmly and sketch out the lines of human experience in postwar Spain. Since they engaged literature and life on the same temporal plane, transmission of the past or conjuring horizons of the future were perceived as contrary to the defined aim of their writing. As a result, the present was firmly inscribed in their narrative and its immediacy sanctified as a homology of the real. In the broadest sense, therefore, the social realists injected literature with a heavy dose of current life, which is a way, of course, of fusing the writing of fiction with the recording of contemporary history.

The purpose and design of social realism in postwar Spain turns upon a small but compelling cluster of assumptions: the belief that objective reality exists and is translatable; the perceived coincidence between the sign and its referent; the assertion that to narrate life is to re-present it in the whole of its authenticity; the notion that a literature committed to social action is able to transform the world into something other than it is. These assumptions, as well as the body of critical writing that has scrutinized them, have generally argued for the primacy of content over form and the eminence of theme over style. Meaning has been determined largely by its degree of social relevance, while technique has been perceived as a secondary contrivance that serves to shape the desired social end. Thus, for example, novels such as Fernández Santos's *Los bravos* (1954) or Caballero Bonald's *Dos días de setiembre* (1961) chronicle how rural poverty destroys the fabric of social relations, while Sánchez Ferlosio's *El Jarama* (1956) or Luis Goytisolo's *Las mismas palabras* (1962) incarnate the perpetual boredom of the young bourgeoisie. The technique used in each case (and in other social realistic novels like them) is viewed as adequate to the task of revealing the reality bracketed by the text, and the assumption persists that meaning is *expressed* or *reflected* by the narrative rather than produced by it. In other words, social realism has acquired the status of a document for literary critics and historians who seek in it a level of performance validated by life itself.

While the word/world correlation implied by both the production and reception of social realism assumes a set of critical values open to debate and even subversion,[3] the recurrent focus on the novel's capacity to represent life suggests an area of inquiry that has remained largely overlooked: the relationship of social realism to the recording of history and to the contingencies of historiography in postwar Spain. I mean by this the way in which the main intentional and performative construct of social realism, the depiction of life "as it really is," is shaped by a deeply embedded concern with the flow of the temporal present and with the way in which the present is perceived and narrated. Every literary text, as Thomas Greene has observed, "expresses or defines by implication a version of history, an implicit theory of history" (266–67). In the case of social realism, history is rendered in a way that simultaneously affirms and negates time. That is to say, the confluence of fictional and historical narration for the social realists hinges upon "historical" circumstances that are experiential rather than narratively reconfigured (time affirmed), and upon a historical past from which the social realists are excluded by a political State that holds the past and its history as its own (time negated). Juan Goytisolo has rightfully noted (even as he rejects many of the premises of social realism) that "the future historian will have to draw upon [the novel of social realism]" if he seeks to understand the historical reality of postwar Spain (*Furgón* 60). My purpose here is to lay out the process through which the novels of social realism detect history and write it into discourse.

The pursuit of intentionality in fiction is rarely a fruitful undertaking.[4] It may constrict potential meaning by privileging the prenarrational authority of the writer, or it may offer up an overtly deterministic meaning that circumscribes the creative role of the reader. But by intentionality in this instance I am not referring to what an author "meant to say" in a given work (i.e., whether a particular novelist set out to criticize the bourgeoisie, the rural poor, or life in the city). I mean instead the quasi-theoretical base (quasi not because it is intellectually thin, but because it was of secondary interest to these writers—unlike, for example, the more recent metafictionists) that gives impetus to the whole enterprise of writing for the social realists and which enunciates the aims of narrative as a form of literary transcription and social action. The following observations by Spanish novelists in a special issue of *Les Lettres Français* in 1962 are representative of the historical intentions of the social realists as a whole:

> *J. M. Caballero Bonald:* It was six or seven years ago when I awakened, like others, to the historical reality of my country. . . . Literature must respond fully to a precise historical reasoning and . . . every work of art must fulfill a specific social role. (4)

> *Juan Marsé:* It is well known that the primary duty of every novelist consists of describing reality without falsifying it. (5)

> *Antonio Ferres:* For me, reality is the only source of a literary work. The form, style, and technique of narration are not born "a priori," but rather are the result of hard work and are determined by the themes, the manner, and the way of seeing them, in short, by the content of the work of art. (5)

> *Alfonso Grosso:* I attempt . . . to make known in other countries the problems of Spain, by means of the shock effect that the reader who is not familiar with authentic Spanish reality may experience. (4)

Luis Goytisolo, in an interview in *Insula* in 1959, declared similar intentions:

> The most important thing is to confront reality, analyze it, almost as a scientist would. . . . So-called intention . . . seems to me to be a fact imposed by reality and, as such, fundamentally objective. ("Responde" 4)

The above comments are of course grounded in such problematic terms as "truth" and "reality," and convey an ingenuous certitude that writing is the equivalent of doing and that words stand equal to the objects they name. But such thinking also evokes a consistent intentionality rooted in a concern for the history of contemporary Spain and, by extension, a concern for how that history will be understood as it is framed in literary discourse.

Beyond the postulates of novelistic intention enunciated by novelists themselves, literary historians and critics have also argued for the historiographic value of social realistic fiction. These arguments have been developed less than systematically and have grown from a variety of critical postures, but all share a declared belief in the historical reliability of social realistic narrative. In her study *Rojos y rebeldes*, for example, Shirley Mangini places social realism squarely within the line of historiography. She points to the "problem of history" (111) as the central concern of the social realists and suggests that their most important contribution is "more historical than literary" (119). Novelist and critic Antonio Ferres has underscored in his essays how the "historical vacuum" (25) in large part motivated the writing of the social realists, while Juan Pedro Quiñonero has summarized the function of these novelists as the inscription into discourse of "the historical reality of the moment" (1). In his book on the novel and postwar culture, Fernando Alvarez Palacios has observed the importance for the social realists "of being and of being *in* their historical moment" (47), while Carlos Barral, less patient with the normative configuration of social realism, has noted how these writers became excessively preoccupied with "rigid dogmatism concerning historical accuracy" (Alvarez Palacio 46). In short, critical thought has long pointed the way for the linking of history and social realism, though the intricacies of such linking and the theoretical mechanisms to draw them out have remained largely undefined.

If we pursue the notion of intentionality as a frame for the discussion of social realism, and if we accept as well the critical judgment that social realism is overrun with the historical, we are confronted by a number of intriguing questions. First of all, from the point of view of literary history, we might inquire why the novels of this period are determinately preoccupied with history. This is not to ask why they are grounded in many of the traditions of Realism, but rather why they fashion their narrative in a way that calls forth assumptions about historical realities. Beyond this we must ask what history means for these writers and how it relates to historiography. Equally pertinent, we must attempt to define the process through which language gains meaning and how it comes to constitute the history that these writers seek to render. We must address in some fashion the fundamental notion that social realism discloses the authentically historical by the way in which it works to mitigate the common distinction in fiction between truth and meaning. And finally, we must attempt to discern the view of narrative held by the social realists that permits them to tell a story of human affairs marked by the flow of time almost wholly in the present, with little concern for temporal distancing, origins, and causation.

In the first place, it must be pointed out that there exists no single, paradigmatic novel of social realism that sets forth the whole range of historical responses to the Regime. Instead these responses emerge from the normative principles of social realism as a whole, which give a determinate coherence to social realistic texts to begin with, and which gain meaning through the recurrent interplay of particular discursive practices. Equally important, it must be understood that the bond with the past for the social realists is always inferential rather than referential. The past assumes presence and meaning through its absence, and sustains present time both through the logical causality of chronological flow and the constitutive elements of storytelling. The social realists never hold up historiography and proclaim its deceit, nor do they claim for themselves the banner of historians. But they stand in a particular relationship with the past that insinuates their own role as historians and endows their discourse with certain functions of historiography. This relationship is largely ironic, but always intentional, because their dialogue with history involves a dynamic response to the past that implies divergence. That is to say, the social realists realign the static structures of myth in order to alter the meaning associated with them, but do so without undoing the mythic paradigm itself. Social realistic writers offer a disruption of the discourse of continuity that gives permanence of meaning to the past, and they suggest as well a causation for the present reality, which is denied by a historiography that was largely the private enterprise of political orthodoxy.[5]

In order to place their narrative in time and to scrutinize the real within a temporal flow, the social realists turned to the present, which could not be dispossessed because it was known through experience rather than narration. But when the social realists transformed the experiential into discourse, it became for them an instrument of power immediately and consistently in conflict with the discourse of the State: it remythified historiography because it posited through dissent the origins of a myth (a myth never present in their writings *as* discourse) that ran against the grain. The synchronic thus superseded the diachronic at the level of surface time (i.e., the present), but at the level of theme the structure of time was firmly anchored in an excluded past. While Franco's historiography sought to present that past as epic, with the concomitant emphasis on evoking admiration for the individual and heroic, the social realists called forth what Paul Ricoeur in another context has termed "the sphere of the horrible" (*Time* 3: 188–89) that circumscribes all of the historical present. Social realistic fiction is thus placed in service of the unforgettable (i.e., countermyths of poverty, isolation, alienation, and the like), which the State plainly set out both to annul and to forget.

Thus when a writer such as José Corrales Egea attacks the social realists for privileging the "current time period," and for their refusal to insert contemporary social reality into "a historical dynamism" (10), he misses the critical point. The historians of the State sought to dispose of the problematic (to forget the unforgettable, in Ricoeur's terms) by forging a discourse that omits discord. The social realists, in contrast, dispute history and mythification through their implication of past time in terms of cause and effect—their narratives of course shape the effect and imply a *certain* cause—and through absence at the level of discourse. Hence the present, rather than emerge as the inevitable or final outcome of a completed history shaped by postapocalyptic order and truth (as the State would have it), becomes in the hands of the social realists the inaugural force of a history that implies a past of divergence and a future of dissent.

Harry Levin once called the literary realist "a professional iconoclast, bent on shattering the false images of his day" (248).[6] There were of course many false images to be shattered by the social realists in Spain during the 1950s. One of the most pervasive of these, as I suggested in chapter 1, is rooted in the Regime's insistence on the heroic foundation of Spanish history. For example, one of the most popular forms of narrative promoted by the State in the early postwar period were biographies advancing the ideological exigencies of fascism and the aristocracy. These not only exalted the performance of great acts carried out by great men, but also sustained a view of history, as Mangini has noted, "according to which history is made by exceptional men, *caudillos* such as Napoleon" (15). Franco himself frequently articulated the importance of the heroic in his regime, both in order to affirm his own attachment to the heroic model and to ensure a discourse of continuity with the past. In a speech in August of 1947, for example, Franco declared, "Everything great that exists in Spain has not been the result of chance: it has been the work of noblemen, saints, and heroes, the fruit of great undertakings, of select minorities, of chosen men" (*Franco* 96). Two years later, in a speech honoring the tenth anniversary of the end of the Civil War, Franco similarly drew forth the heroic underpinning of his victory: "Our victory was the triumph of Spain against the anti-Spain, the heroic reconquest of the Fatherland that was moving headlong down the path of destruction. Therefore, our victory was and is for all men and for all classes of Spain" (*Franco* 21).

These views are pertinent to historical understanding for a number of reasons. Above all, the importance attached to "exceptional men" and "saints and heroes" is closely tied to the essentialist view of Spanish history in which the past is shaped by a cluster of salient traits ("an essential Spain, an essential man, archetypes, a way of being that is inherently Catholic and Spanish" [*Explicación* 56], as Fernando Morán puts it) bound up by the recurrent affirmation of the heroic. This idea is embodied fully in the ennobling of individuals, as suggested above, as well as in the glorifying of the collective whole of Spain as a nation. A typical example of such thinking is found in Santiago Montero Díaz, professor of history at the University of Madrid, who asserted in 1943, "Heroic fate is unrenounceable. The very essence of heroism resides in its unrenounceability. Epic heroes or tragic heroes are not occasionally so, but rather are heroes in substance. They lose their essential nature if they lose their heroic quality. Destiny and vocation are one and the same thing for them. The same fate weighs upon certain peoples. To this race of people Spain belongs" (Rodríguez Puértolas 2:1073–74). More specifically concerning the State and the Falange, Montero Díaz adds, "The very essence of [the Falange] lies in its feeling of responsibility for the History of Spain, in its seeking the remote and heroic solidarity with twenty centuries of History, [in] making itself the depository and modernizer of those two thousand years of Spanish existence" (1075).

Within the context of a historiography of the heroic, the novels of social realism offer a sharp repudiation of the given meaning of Spanish history. Dissent in these novels is bodied forth in two principal ways: (1) through the displacement of the individual at the center of human time; (2) through the vitiation of the collective whole of Spain by placing it within Ricoeur's "sphere of the horrible." Although many novels of social realism function on both of these levels to undermine history (e.g., *Los bravos, El Jarama, Dos días de setiembre*), Camilo José Cela's *La colmena* (1951) is in many ways representative of the process. In the first place, Cela himself identifies the historical intention of the novel in his prologue to the fourth edition: "it is a book of history, not a novel" (15). In large part, however, Cela's comment appears to propose only the centrality of history in his work as a correlative of representational accuracy in the portrayal of present-day Madrid. The novel is set in the early 1940s over a period of a few days and traces the activities of a large number of characters during their daily life. The references to Hitler and World War II give the novel an explicit historical frame, but there appears to be scant concern for laying out the historical dilemmas of postwar Spain beyond the daily agony of hunger, unemployment, and despair. In other words, despite the intentionality of Cela to write history, *La colmena* seems to offer a slice of the real in present time without drawing upon the flow of events in the past that we commonly view as constituting history.

When contextualized amid the historiography of the Regime, however, the focus of *La colmena* as a "historical" novel dramatically shifts. First of all, the importance of temporal flow in the novel is evoked by the idea of "the morning, that morning eternally repeated" (277) that reins in the forward movement of time. That is to say, Cela not only projects future time into the single and unchanging cycle of repetition that forms the present, but also pulls the past into this cycle and strikes at the very heart of Francoist myths. The whole of the novel affirms this posture in a variety of ways. Cela himself notes that *La colmena* "is a novel without a hero" ("A *Mrs. Caldwell*" 977). The double meaning of Cela's assertion stems from its double contextualization: in the purely literary sense, no single character is intended to stand apart from the others as protagonist of the novel; within the frame of historiography, however, the very concept of heroism runs against the grain of postwar depravation. Thus rather than suggest the illustrious continuity of an epic past, as did the Franco regime, *La colmena* calls forth the bathos of the mock epic. The novel is not a tale of great achievements and heroic survival presented to the reader with an eye for the majestic. It does imply, however, that the path of events shaping the present (that is to say, the path of history) can be little more than a debased version of what the Regime holds as historically noble and authentic.

This is perhaps best exemplified by the recurrent figure of Martín Marco. At first glance, Martín appears to stand above the masses and resist the present. He leads a bohemian life on the edge of poverty, criticizes the materialism of the bourgeoisie, and writes poetry on scrap paper lifted from the Bank of Spain. He may even face arrest by the police because his papers are not in proper order. Yet Martín serves a broader purpose in the novel when placed in the context of Francoist historiography. Cela himself makes such a placement when his narrator observes that Martín's most recent published article is entitled "Reasons for the Spiritual Permanence of Isabel the Catholic" (208). The intentions here are plainly ironic. The cult of Isabel la Católica, especially during the early years of the Franco regime, is intended to link Francoist beliefs to the heroic values of the birth of Spain. While Martín Marco's intellectual assertions clearly show he collaborates with the Isabelan myth in the Falangist press, his own life (as well as that of the others at doña Rosa's café) reveals how these values have been deformed within Francoist Spain. Not only do the characters appear fully removed from the spiritual values of Isabel, but any link to these values through temporal causation is erased: "The customers of the cafés are people who believe that things happen because they do, that it's not worth trying to make things right" (23).

A similar corruption of the heroic paradigm marks the Nietzschean bar-owner, Celestino, who ties his life to a noble past through his mock-epic dreams and the reading of epic poems. Celestino is particularly attracted to *romances* (ballads) that "begin as God commands"

(185)—that is, with a panegyric to the Virgin Mary—as well as to the heroic acts of soldiers. For example, after reading the noble words of Corporal Pérez, who requests at his execution to be given a "good death," Celestino exalts, "What a fellow! There were real men in the old days" (186). But the cruel circumstances of Celestino's present represent a pathetic corruption of his epic aspirations. He sleeps on a pull-down bed in the middle of his small bar (named Aurora, after Nietzsche's work); he often serves only a single customer (a policeman who arrests illegal vendors in subway stations); he suffers from the same pervasive decay of postwar poverty and depravation that characterize the patrons of doña Rosa's café. Clearly, Celestino (along with Martín Marco and scores of other characters in similar conditions) is used in *La colmena* to turn the whole notion of the heroic on its head. Rather than ennoble the individual, as did the Regime, *La colmena* places value on the broad sweep of the collective; and rather than deify the heroic, the novel celebrates the mundane and the quotidian. As Sanz Villanueva has observed, Madrid (and Spain, by implication) is most meaningfully viewed in the novel as "the spectacle of a great, collective frustration" (278).

A similar turn from the heroic lies at the root of José Manuel Caballero Bonald's *Dos días de setiembre* (1962). The novel is constructed with the standard social realistic reliance on the collective protagonist—in this instance, characters move about the Andalusian landscape and represent the various economic groups and social concerns of rural postwar Spain. Hunger and unemployment are recurrent subthemes of the novel, and the pervasive poverty of present-day circumstances is tied to the past (i.e., things have always been this way) through the cyclical pattern of the harvest and other natural elements. The levantine winds and approaching storm urge the novel toward a structural conclusion, at the same time intensifying the mythical repetition of decay and social injustice.

The most forceful undercutting of the heroic in the novel turns upon the dichotomy between the rich (don Andrés and don Gabriel, both wealthy landowners) and the poor (most notably Joaquín, an unemployed worker) in the context of postwar persecution and exploitation. The Franco regime, as we have seen, sought to legitimate its full integration into Spanish history by constructing an epic past of meaningful figures and events. Its central icons were noble and heroic and were endowed with a spiritual completeness. Caballero Bonald perturbs the epic history of the Regime by locating all of his characters within the circle of postwar antipathies and by implying a causal relationship between past and present. Both Andrés and Gabriel serve as prime examples—they exert political and economic control over the area and reinforce the sphere of the horrible that circumscribes the novel. Andrés, for example, owes his wealth to inheritance. Although there is nothing damning or even peculiar about inheritance in general, the whole of his life controverts any hint of nobility. In the first place, as a youth he succeeded in avoiding military service by claiming extreme susceptibility to heat. In other words, he was a coward. Furthermore, his entire character is developed in the novel to show material and physical weaknesses, all of which underscore his effeminate affectations. Since he has been engaged in little but accumulating wealth through scant effort of his own ("The money . . . had multiplied on its own, without don Andrés knowing exactly in what quantity and for what reasons" [35]), and since his original wealth is attached to the past ("Don Andrés, the only son, inherited . . . an old, accumulated fief of vineyards and pastures" [35]), Andrés's recurrent presence in the novel coaxes effeteness to the forefront of history: his lineage suggests continuity between a past and present marked only by decay.

The same holds true for don Gabriel. The rich landowner is a selfish and materialistic tyrant (a "fat cow," as he is called) intimately bound up with social injustice. This is revealed most directly through contrast with Joaquín, whose accidental death gives dramatic poignancy to the novel. Joaquín in particular stands out against the backdrop of workers because he has a clear sense of the present framed by the past: he fought at the Málaga front in 1937 on the Republican side, was imprisoned after the war, and was later denied documentation that would permit him to work. Joaquín's conflict with the mayor of his hometown, and later with Gabriel, gains stark concretion in the leitmotif of decay that Joaquín envisions at the core of postwar life:

And now the stubborn and pitiless night had fallen, fetid and sweltering with mud oozing a miserable heaviness in every corner of the village, foul-smelling, permeating every bitter stream of saliva, every vomited puddle of stum. . . . [And] on the other side, toward the warehouses, the night also was gathering in the nauseating ferment of the wine and the decay of wood from the barrels, excavating the little crystals of glucose and the burning strias of alcohol, molding the final bits of bread with the manure of the drinking trough. (250)

The smells of fermentation and decay are deeply embedded in the everyday existence of the town, and their juxtaposition to the diachronic patterns of harvest and weather compels a coalescence of past and present. This coalescence implies sameness across time—the (absent) past clearly emerges as precursor, the present as consequence, and the final triumph of stasis obliterates the possibility of change in the future. In this way the meanings of the historical myths of the Regime are discredited, but without erasing their basic mythic structure. Hence in Caballero Bonald's view, the Franco regime does not represent the culmination of a heroic and noble historical process begun with Isabel la Católica and the reconquest of Spain from the infidels. Rather it embodies the perversion of such a process. In the context of Francoist historiography, *Dos días de setiembre* argues forcefully for the exclusion of the individual hero in the historical frame of postwar Spain, and it thereby vitiates the essentialist posturing of historians of the Regime.

A similar scheme of mythic reversal shapes the role of the Church in the novels of social realism. For historians of the Regime, as I have shown, the Church stood at the very heart of the birth of Spain as a nation. Equally important, it sustained the country's moral superiority in modern Europe even as Spanish material power steadily eroded. The Regime's historians sanctified the moral and spiritual authority embodied by the Church so that it became crucial to the myth of an eternal Spain as well as to the more concrete precepts of power assumed by the State in the present. This is perhaps most succinctly encapsulated in Manuel García Morente's lapidary assertion in 1945 that "One cannot be Spanish and not be Catholic" (Rodríguez Puértolas 2:994), an idea, as we have seen, that is deeply embedded in the historiography of Menéndez y Pelayo as well as the historians who propagated his ideas for the State.

While there is no clear paradigmatic role assigned to Catholicity in the novels of social realism, both the function and power of the Church are generally vitiated through the figure of the local priest. The priest in fact often emerges as the metonymic agent for controverting the essentialist myth that identifies what is Spanish with what is Catholic. Of course, the portrayal of corrupt priests and illicit activities of the Church has a long and vital history in Spanish fiction, from *Lazarillo de Tormes* to the novels of Juan Goytisolo.[7] But what is particularly striking in many of the novels of social realism is not the rebuke of greed and corruption, as might be expected, but rather that the Church appears as a hollow, shadowy presence whose once powerful hold on Spanish society has become radically diminished. That is to say, rather than assume a central role in the quotidian affairs of the town and the spiritual life of the people, as it once did, the Church has become detached from daily living and relegated to the minor functions of celebration. This is perhaps most dramatically portrayed in the rural novels of Jesús Fernández Santos. In *En la hoguera* (1957), for example, the town no longer has a priest of its own and the church doors are opened only a few days a year (127–28). Similarly in *Los bravos* (1954), the small rural town is marked by a pervasive disintegration that reaches into religious myth through the decayed church, symbol of the town's eternal and inescapable ruin: "The emptiness surrounding the blackened ruins of the church, on the very edge of the town, became visible, and could even be smelled" (12); "The church was empty, its walls bare, covered with ferns and thistles, and only occasionally did the priest come up from the other town, twenty kilometers away" (105).

Even when the priest visits these towns, however, he remains apart, and serves only to buttress the foundation of Fernández Santos's countermythic vision of spiritual decay. In *Los bravos* the priest is identified with the traveling con artist who has swindled the townspeople of their money: "From underneath the cassock there appeared blue pants and old, dirty shoes that reminded the woman of the traveler" (126). From the perspective of the priest, the townspeople scarcely merit the spiritual vigilance of the Church. "[The priest] asked himself if there was anything good about that town, among those poor, miserable people. . . . It was a poor town, and in its poverty it endured its punishment" (123). The Church thus appears to function merely as an adjunct to the town, whose base of power now lies with the wealthy landowners. Yet through the presence / absence paradox, the Church is crucial to the historical vision offered by the novel. If at the core of Spanish history lies the myth of Catholicity and its spiritual strength, Fernández Santos shows here not the destruction of the myth, but its reconfiguration, sustained fully by absence and impotence. Not only has the Church abandoned the town to its decay, thereby engendering the reversal of its mythic role, but God himself is now excluded. As the narrator remarks in *En la hoguera*, the ringing of the church bell underscores only that "God is going to die, that God has died" (147). It is in this way that Fernández Santos places the Church in Ricoeur's sphere of the horrible and fashions for the flow of history a radical alternative to the eternal grace of Catholicity set forth by the Regime.

Thus far I have focused largely on the intention of social realism with respect to the portrayal of the real and the subversion of postwar historiography. I turn now to the practical functioning of social realism as a mode of narration and suggest ways in which technique and language ally it with the writing of history as a narrative discipline, rather than exclusively with the historiography characteristic of early postwar Spain.[8] First, however, it is necessary to return briefly to the discussion of time.

The location of narrative time in the present in social realistic fiction is important for several reasons. First of all, one of the central elements of historiography turns upon its implicit hypothesis of temporal flow. As Ricoeur suggests, the "Realist" hypothesis (which shapes postwar social realism) places its chronological determinations on a single scale of time often referred to as "history of the earth" (*Time* 3: 181). In terms of narration, this hypothesis reveals a reciprocal borrowing between historians and novelists and establishes for the two disciplines a symmetry of form and potential meanings. The time scale involves connecting different points of the chronological flow within a particular narration so that what are perceived as points of commonality may be endowed with the elements of common meaning. This view of time in fact is how the narrative of history professes to portray the real as it unfolds in time. As Ricoeur puts it, the "reinscription of the time of narrative within the time of the universe with a single time scale [the human scale] marks the specificity of the referential mode characteristic of historiography" (*Time* 3: 181). To reinscribe the past within narrative, of course, calls forth the historian's historical imagination. Historians must transport themselves into an alien moment and, drawing upon documents, archives, and other materials, create a figure of that moment with words. This process embodies what Hayden White refers to as the representative function of history, through which historians implicate and proclaim that what they have represented is what they would have witnessed if they had been present to observe the events as they occurred.

The temporal/referential coupling undertaken by historians is closely aligned with the thinking of the social realists, but is relevant to their narrative in more intense ways because of their insistence on representing the present not "as if" they had been there, but specifically as witnessed and lived time. The overriding hierarchy of social realism in terms of narration, therefore, is informed less by its social, political, or economic content than by its firm attachment to a particular view of time. The deep meaning of the historical in social realism, in fact, emerges in relation to what may be termed its "chronotope."[9] Used extensively by Bakhtin to draw out the complexities of form in the novel, "chronotope" means literally "time-space," and refers in social realism to the way in which temporal and spatial components are connected within narration. In social realism, this connection always privileges the temporal through the recurrent irony of stasis. That is to say, while the spatial frame of social realism is expansive within the Iberian Peninsula (e.g., Andalucía in *Campos de Níjar*, León in *Los bravos*, Barcelona in *Las mismas palabras*, Madrid in *El Jarama*), the temporal focus remains fixed always in the present and insinuates the crucial determinant of repetition. History here is therefore displayed on two levels. First, the social realists challenge the notion (as did Heidegger) that temporal distance is a necessary component of historiography. They thus set aside oldness as having primordial significance. Second, and most pertinent, the very idea of the past casts a shadow on the present through the play of paradox: the shadow of the missing. Social realists indeed argue for the authoritative presence of the present, but they assume as well equal significance for the absent past.

Since the past in postwar Spain belongs to the State, the presentness of social realism opens to conflict the whole notion of temporal continuity. Historians of the Regime, of course, are caught up in an oxymoronic dilemma: they at once attach the present to the past, so that the present emerges apodictically from a heroic and Catholic history, and they deny the principle of continued historical flow, which has now reached fruition (and therefore has ceased) in the postapocalyptic and posthistorical time of Franco. In other words, historians of the Regime exalt the continuity of Spain's authentic past at the same time that they peremptorily assert that such a relation no longer obtains. As Fernando Morán puts it, for these historians the past is "truncated by the claim that society has entered into a new order, that it has left behind its prehistory or that it has returned to an ideal, full, and harmonious time" (*Explicación* 30). For Francoist historians, as we have seen, this "ideal time" is pre-Reformation Europe and the perceived permanence of Catholic spirituality embodied by the Spain of the Reconquest. The essential value of this Spanish past is expelled from prominence following the Middle Ages, only to be repossessed in the present as part of the ideal time of myth. The present time of the Regime thus becomes, as Morán acutely puts it, "The time of the end of all time" (22).

Within this context of temporal stasis (or postapocalyptic truth, as the Regime would have it), social realists build their countermyths in a present time that calls forth unremitting chronological flow, but does so through the agency of circular repetition. Hence as with Francoist historiography, this fiction advances the proposition that temporal flow has ceased. But the cluster of oxymoronic principles that impels Spanish historiography (the recurrent coupling of past and present and circularity, versus the cessation of time and stasis) is rearticulated in social realism to engender a fundamentally different *meaning* for Spanish history. The mythic structures of narration remain largely intact, but the reversal of focus transfers the meaning of history from the sphere of the admirable to the sphere of the horrible.

This can be readily seen, for example, in Caballero Bonald's *Dos días de setiembre*, which is imbued with temporality as stasis. It is not that time has ceased to exist for the characters in the novel, but that its leadenness disallows change. The following brief dialogue illustrates how characters typically perceive the passing of time as the conjugate of stagnation:

"It has been a long time since you've come."
"Quite a while," said Miguel.
"More than a year."

"Something like that."

"The last time was the same. . . . Do you remember?"

"The same. Around here the only thing that changes is the skin of the snakes." (53)

Later the narrator notes concerning Miguel that "[h]e felt a lot older than he really was, as if he had finished living the gloomiest part of his life and now he had to painfully make his way along the difficult terrain of a dark and dying time without the slightest sign of hope" (289). The characters in both of these instances experience fully the continual flow of time, but the absence of change affirms the underlying mythic principle in social realistic narration of time affirmed and time negated. This principle (which of course is not only temporal but narrative in nature) gains breadth of meaning for social realistic fiction when set alongside the broadly held view among historians that, as Peter Munz writes, "History, as the science of change, [is] concerned with the succession of events" (22). In other words, the sequencing of events in social realistic novels parallels the formative narrative strategies of historians in a general way, so that past and present are intimately bound up with one another—they exist in a relationship of causality within the chronological flow of time. More directly related to historians of the Regime, the novels of social realism also advance the paradox of temporal flow and stagnation. In the context of historical narrative, social realism offers the implicit message that an admirable past of heroism and nobility is precluded by a present in which such traits are strikingly absent. In this way the weight of the past gains full presence in the present through the fundamental principle of temporal and narrative sequencing and the logic of causality.

But the implications of narrative sequencing and chronology do not end here—they are also projected into the future. As the narrator of *Dos días de setiembre* notes concerning Lola:

Lola, with time, allowed herself to be overcome by listlessness, growing used to the idea that it wasn't worth taking care of herself and watching her figure. She didn't imagine that she could possibly struggle against that sort of crafty moth that tenaciously and unconsciously was gnawing at the weakened foundation of her feelings. Lola was vegetating, scarcely realizing what she was doing and what she had stopped doing, resigning herself instinctively to her lethargy. (99–100)

The unheroic past and present preclude all hope for change in the future. This idea of course embodies the postapocalyptic stasis envisioned by Francoist historiography, but turns the meaning of the static on its head. Rather than stand comfortably amid the revealed truth of the Francoist victory, time now languishes and turns back on itself to produce abulia and decay.

This same sense of time pervades many other novels of social realism as well. In *Los bravos*, for example, the stopping of temporal flow is pointedly represented by the image of the clock on the church tower: "The clock appeared motionless—it was missing its hands—in an unreal time" (12). The "unreal time" here, of course, is fully the time of myth. When located amid the spatial composition of the town (ruins of the church, crumbling walls, emptiness), time emerges to convey its destructive contradiction: temporal flow has ceased, yet the decay intimately associated with time persists. This is further underscored in the novel through narrative structure. It is a truism of social realistic fiction that the end of the narration (both in time and in structure) grows from the beginning. This allows the story to move through time in "real-life" sequencing. There is also the sense that this temporal movement projects toward a future—something happens that leads a character (or characters) from one state of being to another. In *Los bravos*, however, while time flows inexorably, it leads only to stasis and repetition. This is most acutely exemplified through the story of the newly arrived doctor (whose name we never learn) and don Prudencio, the wealthy landowner. Prudencio has held power over the town for decades, but is now old and vulnerable to change. During the course of the novel the doctor gradually chooses to live as an outcast within the village at the same time that he moves to co-opt the authority of Prudencio: he gains possession of Socorro (Prudencio's mistress); he opposes the town (as only Prudencio had done before) by helping a swindler escape the townspeople's wrath; when Prudencio dies, he assumes control of the landowner's large house. Early in the novel we learn that Prudencio enjoyed sitting on the balcony of his house, where he could view the town below: "From the semidarkness behind the venetian blind, he could see the town at his feet, the double row of houses on both sides of the river, springing up from the brown dry earth" (83). In precisely the same fashion at the end of the novel the doctor positions himself on the balcony: "The doctor went out on the balcony. He pulled up a chair and, sitting down, contemplated the town at his feet" (236). Through these and other parallels between the two characters, the end of the story returns the reader to the very beginning. The inhabitants of the town will continue to be dominated by the figure in the big house and will endure a life of resignation and hatred. Placed beside the cyclical time of Francoist historiography, this cycle of "return" in *Los bravos* shows how the mythic paradigm holds firmly in place, but its meaning is now fully circumscribed by the sphere of the horrible. The past thus stands dissociated from heroism, and the future bears no hope for change because the mythic time of decay has revealed its meaning as an eternal tragedy.

Such a view is commonly buttressed in other novels of social realism as well. In Cela's *La colmena*, as I have shown, the narrator evokes "the morning, that morning eternally repeated" (277); in Luis Goytisolo's *Las mismas palabras*, the narrator establishes temporal stasis in the first sentence by portraying numbing repetition: "The same words, the same gestures, everything happened again the same as before" (25); in Sánchez Ferlosio's *El Jarama* the epigraph by da Vinci ("The water that we touch in the rivers is the last of what has gone and the first of what is to come; thus the present") underscores the constant flow of the river that comes to be identified with myth and repetition. Each of these novels projects not a heroic time marked by great events, but what Sánchez Ferlosio has called a "common time" (Villanueva, '*El Jarama*' 50) that places time and its implacable passage within the sphere of the horrible. These novels embody Américo Castro's countermythic view of Spain as "un vivir desviviéndose" and thus stand acutely opposed to the mythic time of revelation attached by the Regime to the pre-Reformation spirituality of an essential and eternal Spain.

It is not, therefore, that the social realists deny the notion of continuity within the flow of time; in fact their narrative implies it always. As I have sought to show, the temporal present of social realism assumes a past that inevitably precedes the reality of that present within the frame of continuity—a past that precludes the heroic and individual. The characters and events laid out in the present are utterly ordinary, and they embody a sense of historical time as repetition and sameness. Thus through the implication of structure, the present emerges from the past and contains the past within it. The emphasis on present time, of course, enables the social realists to avoid the historian's dilemma of reenactment as a temporal problem. Still, the two share the more fundamental predicament of constructing a narrative in time that renders the course of events as they are perceived to be.

The portrayal of life "as it really is," it will be remembered, is the articulated aim of the social realists, and this aim imposes a view of narration and language that compels novelists to assert a firm hold on reality and truth. Yet the dilemma for these writers, as for all writers whose task is sanctioned by perceptions of the real, is inescapable: all discourse shapes and defines—rather than reflects—the nature of meaning in the events (real or make-believe) that it sets out to relate. This holds true for the world of the chivalric romance on the one hand, as well as for the narrative of the most fact-based book of history on the other. Thus through the agency of narration, the social realists clearly stand proximate to the historian. To show how this is so, it is necessary to disclose the recurrent strategies of narration that shape the real in social realistic discourse.

In the first place, the social realists set out to be "objective" in their novels. Such an aim overtly engages a convention of realistic writing and has little to do with the philosophical issue of objectivity, the subject, and the self. But it is a convention nonetheless highly charged with strategies which, while vulnerable to parody and subversion, carry forth the meanings associated with that tradition. For example, the use of the third-person impersonal narrator, which consistently functions as the preferred mode of narration in social realism, produces the illusion of pure reference. It is of course an illusion, the effect of one rhetorical device chosen from a range of potential voices. But third-person narration seems able to suffuse discourse with what Henry James has called "the intensity of illusion" (Ricoeur, *Time* 3: 161). For the social realists, the technique effectively reduces mimesis to imitation and brings to the fore the symmetry between narrative strategy and concern for the truth. The third-person narrator provokes the illusion of presence through imitation and thus authenticates the equivalence between "seeing as" (the perception of reality) and "being as" (the onto-logical force of the narrative). This approximation of voice and voiced serves a dual purpose: (1) it places meaning and truth on the same plane; (2) when coupled with the intensive effect of present time, it enables social realistic narration to bridge traditional distinctions between the real and the unreal (i.e., between history and fiction) and to place at the center of narration a historicized rendering of life.

The novels of social realism thus stand in contrast to the important works of the 1940s, such as Camilo José Cela's *La familia de Pascual Duarte* (1942) and Carmen Laforet's *Nada* (1945), even though these novels convey many of the social concerns of the time. Narrated in the first person, these works most often give their accounts the generic feeling of a memoir. The narrators are to be mistrusted, not because they set out to lie or to evade the truth, but because the nature of their evocation relies upon memory, and thus upon the aporias of time as antecedent. For Spanish writers of memory following the period of social realism (e.g., Juan Goytisolo, Luis Goytisolo, Martín Gaite), distance is traversed in the belief that time can disperse nothing without the possibility that the mind will reconstruct it as a vital component of the present. Time lost thus becomes equated with time regained. For the social realists, in contrast, the notion of "having been" skews the real. The past is not observable but *memorable,* and thus desynchro-nizes third-person discourse in the strategies of storytelling and at the level of truth.

The defining principle of the social realists for telling their stories turns upon the notion of "followability." As with all writers of narrative (although the historians of the Regime asserted the contrary through their belief in a universal history embedded in the "facts"), the social realists do not "receive" the discourse and the events related within it, but rather make decisions about such things as beginnings, middles, and ends, the sequential logic of the narration, and the principle of cause and effect. The compendium of decisions made by the social realists eventually forms the paradigmatic structure of their writing—the common model or story type for explaining the contingencies of present-day life. The events chosen to be represented, those "histor-ical" events included in the narrative, are in themselves value neutral. The value they eventually obtain, then, hinges upon the configuration given them. And it is precisely the historical view implicit in the canons of the social realists that defines their strategies of configuration.

In large part, the social realists view history as a set of what Hayden White has called "dispersed entities" (*Tropics* 63). What they relate (e.g., the dangerous working conditions of miners in *En la hoguera,* the poverty of farmers or the lack of housing in *Dos días de setiembre*) results from an analytical operation that stops short of establishing explicit laws of causation but which suggests temporal precedence for the actual through the repetition of analogous events within the story to be told. For historians who adhere to such a view, a field of study is revealed, as White shows, "to be a set of essentially autonomous particulars subsumable under no general rule" (*Tropics* 63). Following closely this line of thought, the social realists configure their narratives less as episodic than as diffuse. This allows for a loose arrangement of plot materials and the dispersion of story components within a single temporal plane. What is narrated, of course, must be perceived as congruent with the elements that are co-opted from life and grasped together in a form that appears adequate to the reality they convey. Like historians, the social realists place value on followability and eschew abstractions that stand in the way of their narrative paradigm. In large part, their narrative is aimed at limiting the possibility of awkward questions and at suggesting an integrity of explanation. And as Frank Kermode points out, followability also permits the writer to sustain the important illusion of third-person narration that "felicitous assertion equals accurate reference" (*Secrecy* 117). Hence the notion that history and fiction share narrative paradigms impels the basic technique of the social realists and determines the parameters for their representation of the real.

One of the institutional beliefs that social realists share with historians is the view that language not only has a hold on the world, but that it can account for the world's complexities. In absolute terms, of course, such a posture is ingenuous, as structuralist and poststructuralist theory has sought with some success to explain. But the word/world coupling by the social realists suggests another level of sense, one that requires the recognition of opacity, transparency, and metaphor. The commingling of these ideas motivates the basic strategies of representation for social realism and allows it as well to claim authenticity at the level of history. First of all, the social realists display scant linguistic self-consciousness. For this reason critics have generally concluded that language functions for social realism as a transparent vehicle of representation. In other words, social realists are generally viewed as speaking plainly, as using language to nail things in their place. Such a view explicitly refuses to engage language as autonomous or self-referential, and generally frees itself from the need to question the myriad of ways in which language can work. While the above characterization of language in social realism can be held as true at the level of both intention and tradition (and thus allows social realism to approximate the communicative strategies of historiography), it is a view that overlooks discourse as metaphor and, equally important, ignores the way in which social realism contests the monologism of the discourse of the State.

Above all, language for the social realists is useful. Words serve not only to open the world to meaning beyond language (i.e., words make the world present to the reader), but to reveal the emptiness of discourse coerced and dispersed by the State. Juan Goytisolo's passionate admonition to attack the Franco regime through the subversion of its language is validated by his own discourse of dissent beginning with *Señas de identidad* in 1966,[10] and can be detected in the subsequent novels of Benet, Martín Gaite, Cela, and Delibes, among others. Certainly, the rejection of language in its narrow range of use by the social realists eventually helped to reinvigorate the Spanish novel and to produce more complicated modes of narration. But it was a posture that failed to account for two compelling principles: (1) the metaphorical root of all narrative fiction; and (2) the way in which the discourse of social realism functions through irony and paradox to undercut not the truth, but the *value* of all that it represents and holds to be authentic in Francoist Spain.

The paradox of language is particularly crucial to the claim for truth in social realism. By paradox I mean how the tension of social realism obtains through the shuttling back and forth between what is transparent at the level of reference and what is opaque at the level of meaning. Both the metaphorical and the intertextual come to bear on this process as it relates to the historical. As I have shown, the historiography sanctioned by the Regime during the 1940s and 1950s was largely epic in scope and heroic in intent. It co-opted the past and bound it to myths that declared the logic of inevitable progression at the expense of dissent and diversity. This process can be seen not only at the level of meaning, but on the correlative surface of linguistic authority in the State's pursuit of a common language. As Bakhtin puts it, "Unitary language constitutes the theoretical expression of the historical processes of linguistic unification and centralization, an expression of the centripetal forces of language. A unitary language is not something given [*dan*] but is always in essence posited [*ʒadan*]—and at every moment of its linguistic life it is opposed to the realities of heteroglossia" (270).

When Max Aub complains that the style of Spanish narrative during the 1950s is "administrative Castilian" (Conte 1), he is of course lamenting, in Bakhtin's words, the absence of a "genuine heterology." But while Aub speaks incisively to the point of contention, he undervalues the intentionality of discourse. The social realists make the language of their narrative so deeply common, so utterly transparent, that we remain largely unaware of its presence even as we gather together meaning from what it says. It indeed "says" something about life (rural towns are isolated, Spanish youths are bored, fishermen are starving, etc.), but it also says something about itself. Language in all its commonness is revealed as unified and centralized and therefore void of meaning-as-truth. In this sense, the narrative of social realism stands as an intimate joining of form and content: it is an empty language used both to represent and to embody an empty existence. But at the level of history, in the hands of the social realists this language (i.e., the common language propagated by the State) is infused with tension. It speaks against the myths of the Regime (conquest, liberation, heroism, and the like) in the language of the Regime, and in doing so lays bare the deceit of its own homogeneous discourse. Social realism thus functions ironically, as I suggested earlier, to remythify Spanish history. It establishes a base for understanding the historical by positing a reality in the present that necessitates a past vastly divergent from the official one.

It is in this sense that the narrative of social realism speaks metaphorically. Certainly, the social realists (as well as historians) use metaphors in their narrative, but these have little to do with the metaphorical as I mean it here. Discourse as metaphor refers in this instance to the way in which language points in two directions at the same time: toward the reality described in the narration and toward a discourse or myth that postwar culture (and in particular, historiography) has made familiar and imposed as valid.[11] In the case of the social realists, negativity becomes the principal impetus for understanding this metaphoric function. That is to say, the view of history and narrative proposed by the social realists is generated through contrast with the prevailing norms of historiography and the myths that pertain to this historiography. Rather than the past, the social realists focus on the present; rather than the epic, the mock epic; rather than the individual, the collective; and rather than the heroic, the quotidian. The importance of this divergence can be perceived fully only if we see how the narrative of social realism points to the world on the one hand, while on the other it reveals the disjunction at the level of meaning with the style that it assumes. Understood in this way, the language of social realism participates fully as a determinant in the circulation of linguistic codes that constitute the real. The metaphorical functioning of the discourse is thus fully adequate to the intentionality of the social realists, since the reference is split toward the reality of the living and the narrative of history. This "split referencing" can be viewed as the primordial reference, as Ricoeur puts it in another context, "to the extent that it suggests, reveals, unconceals . . . the deep structures of reality to which we are related as mortals who are born into this world and who dwell in it for a while" ("Metaphorical Process" 151).

The enriching potential of split-referentiality, then, motivates the narrative of social realism both through intention and through performance. Social realistic fiction arose at least in part in response to a historiography that consistently deferred the convergence of truth and meaning, and sought to put in its place a discourse of imitation that stood as the equal of truth. The social realists never intended to reconfigure the past as discourse, but to sketch its imprint by insinuating a past knowable through the sequencing of cause and effect and temporal continuity. It was a way of fighting for memory without evoking the aporias of time (or, in a more practical vein, without evoking the ire of censorship), a way of salvaging time and maintaining history in its full temporal breadth coiled beneath the surface of the present. Social realism can thus be perceived as both revealing and transforming, and stands firmly opposed to the postapocalyptic tranquility advanced by historians of the Regime. It reveals in the sense that it draws to light truths that were concealed by the discourse of historiography but already sketched out at the heart of experience. It transforms in the sense, as Ricoeur shows, "that a life examined in this way is a changed life, another life" (*Time* 3: 158). Of course, social realistic fiction did not metamorphose postwar Spain, but it did give rise to the exigence to think differently about the present and about the past that implicates it. Social realism evoked and preserved Ricoeur's "another life," and it is this life in its full range of alternatives that stands as the most important contribution of social realistic fiction.

3

History and the Novel

of Memory

Dissonance

(if you are interested)

leads to discovery.

—William Carlos Williams,

Paterson IV

What the historiographic discourse of the Regime achieved by myth-ifying the past in the sphere of the admirable, and what the social realists grafted upon the past through mythic counterpoint in Ricoeur's sphere of the horrible, is eroded and dispersed during the 1960s and 1970s by the novels of memory. By novels of memory I mean, in the largest sense, those fictions in which past time is evoked through sub-jective remembering, most often by means of first-person narration but not held exclusively to that perspective.[1] The past that is explored in each case (the external referent of the text) is the past largely eschewed or appropriated by historiography under Franco, the lived past of the Civil War and the strains of dissent that anticipate the conflict and persist in its aftermath. It is important to point out, however, that as was the case with the novels of social realism, I am not overtly concerned with what is conveyed in these novels as content (i.e., I am not trying to show that memory distorts concrete facts or that it reveals a particular truth about the past in the "real" world, even though this may indeed be the case). My aim instead is to lay out the process through which the novel of memory detects and makes the past discernible through the contingencies of its discourse.[2]

Though by no means single-voiced in its propositions or tied to a precise set of literary canons, the novel of memory includes those fictions in which the individual self seeks definition by commingling the past and present through the process of remembering. This process may be activated either voluntarily or involuntarily, but in the novels to which I refer, it turns consistently upon a bimodal correlation: the self in search of definition, the definition of self perceived always within the flow of history. History thus stands preeminent in these novels: it places the individual in "real" time and serves as well as a backdrop against which characters emerge, ideas are conveyed, and beliefs posited or disaffirmed. While any of these functions may be played out in the novel of memory, history emerges most resonantly as what Hayden White terms "the content of the form." It is offered both as a consequence of memory and as the originator of memory; it gives meaning to the narrative and structures that meaning. Above all, however, history occupies the narration in a way that subverts the structured tautness of mythic discourse and advances in its place the contingencies of time and meaning. The novel of memory clearly stands with social realism in opposing the historiography of the Regime. In contrast to social realistic fiction, however, it strips history of its structured oneness, of its mythical enactment of progression, and most importantly, of its discourse that disaffirms dissent in the narrative capturing of the past.

Prose fiction (and art in general, as Gadamer has shown) mediates by self-assertion rather than self-effacement. This is especially the case in the novel of memory, but in an ironic sense, since what is asserted is actually the impossibility of narrative assertion. On the one hand, the novel of memory reveals (and asserts) its own determinants at the level of form, and thus lays bare the contingencies of narration as a way of knowing the past. On the other hand, however, the novel of memory is self-effacing in the content of its form, in what it proposes about the discourse of history. In contrast to the single-voiced discourse of myth that shapes social realism and Francoist historiography, and in contrast as well to the assertion of authority of this discourse over the real and the meaning of the real, the novel of memory offers a different claim upon history and its truths. This claim is propositional rather than assertive because it recognizes that to know the historical is to mediate and to narrate it with the voice of a subject in the present who is positioned both within history and within discourse. If one of the proclaimed truths of human existence is that "being" means always being in time, it is a derivative but no less cogent conclusion that we are also in history—we belong to history. Further, as Dilthey suggests, the only way to be objective about history is not to objectify it, not to devise a subject/object dualism that plays out the myths of a univocal epistemology.[3] This is done always and already within the sense-giving strategies implicit in narration, which turn upon the virtuality of a narrator (a "self" in the novels of memory), language, and time. If we view history as the "inherence of time in language," as Jonathan Morse proposes (2), then it is clear that memory becomes the vehicle for defining and fulfilling historical desire. History must therefore be seen not merely as a vocabulary laced into a single discursive paradigm (as with myth), but as the undulation of time captured by a system of words. This system, as I have suggested, is propped against a narrating self in pursuit not of truth but of meaning.

In the novel of memory in postwar Spain, therefore, history does not stand outside of individual consciousness as a form imposed, but rather impinges upon the consciousness of characters and forces its way into their considerations. History supervenes against the discourse of myth in these novels because it both shapes and is shaped by the private affairs of the self. In a practical sense, the most transparent manifestation of this reciprocity appears in the mechanisms of plot. While the social realists transferred life to literature through the principles of logical causality and narrative followability (i.e., past events accumulate to present consequences), the novels of memory turn upon what Lennard Davis in another context has called "teleogenic" plots—the ordering of action and information that "implies the transformation of past events by subsequent ones" (213). The novelists of social realism generally conceive narration as reporting the real through a temporal unfolding that leads to an inevitable conclusion (not in a deterministic sense, but in a narrative one). The novel of memory, in contrast, unravels the plot of the past and transforms the potential for historical knowledge into a web of relations and interactions between the self and history. The narrative of memory thus works on two levels in its teleogenic plotting: (1) its fragmented composition compels the reader to reconfigure the design of followability through the evocation of a past that is not static, but dynamic and ever changing; (2) the external referent of the narrative, the history of Spain, is now an internal component of the self, and is thus open to re-formation as the individual claims authority *not* over truth but against myth.

The teleogenic plotting of history is perhaps most purposefully exemplified in Carmen Martín Gaite's *El cuarto de atrás* (1978). The narrator / protagonist of the book, a fictive Martín Gaite, shuttles back and forth in time during the course of the narrative, and the reflections she offers on her past are intimately bound up with the past of Spain. Her temporal divagations lead her first to contemplate the stultifying myths of Franco's historiography, then to perceive how she has been deprived of history: "At the time I scorned history, and furthermore, I didn't believe a word of what was recounted in history books or in the newspapers" (48); "I would sit myself down on the green sofa opposite this sideboard and look at the saints in the history book, neither glorious exploits nor exemplary conduct struck me as trustworthy models of behavior. Kings who stirred up wars, conquistadors and heroes disturbed me. I was suspicious of their prideful attitude as they set foot in foreign territory, defended forts, or planted crosses and flags" (91). Martín Gaite clearly rejects here the historiographic myths of the Regime, especially those that blanket truth with meanings closed both to exegesis and to dissent.

The myth of Isabel la Católica serves as a highly pertinent example in *Cuarto*. In the same way that Martín Marco in *La colmena* writes to affirm the spiritual permanence of the Catholic queen in the Spain of 1943, or the historians of the Regime exalt her as visionary mother who gave birth to Spain and its empire and who cast pureness as the coequal of Spanishness, Martín Gaite locates Isabel at the center of the Francoist configuration for narrating the past. Above all, Carmen (the narrator) recalls the imposition of childhood values by the state as a correlative of

Isabelan virtue: "We were placed beneath her advocacy, we were given talks about her iron will and her spirit of sacrifice, we were told how she had held the ambition and the despotism of the nobles in check, how she had created the Holy Office, expelled the traitorous Jews, given up her jewels to finance the most glorious undertaking in our history" (89). The narrator here evokes the myths of Isabel not to embrace them as a frame for truth (as does the Regime), but to expose them as a paradigm for deceit forged by the government. Even the memory of the portrait of Isabel is tied to the Regime's constriction of the past. The severe image of the queen in illustrated schoolbooks diminishes her physical attractiveness for the young Carmen, but the image is employed by the schools to confirm the righteousness of Isabel's role in Spanish history. The smile that is pointedly absent from her face becomes for the school a mark of the forbearance and certitude of her authority. It is also a reification of absolute truth: "Happiness was a reward for having done one's duty and was the diametrical opposite of doubt. . . . Queen Isabel never gave herself a moment's respite, never doubted" (89–90).

But Carmen in the present, conjuring up the past, is now too astute not to doubt Francoist truths, hence she reflects upon the deceit of the historiographic discourse that has shaped those truths: "I keep thinking, as I listen to him, of Isabel la Católica, of the deceptive version of her conduct put before us in those textbooks and those speeches, where no room was left for chance, where each step, journey, or decision of the queen appeared to bear the mark of a superior and inevitable destiny" (98). The more fundamental issue here, of course, is Carmen's discovery not of the so-called facts about Isabel, but of the nature of time and memory as they coalesce to establish the contingencies of historical truth. In the end she willingly accedes to the dismantling of the Isabelan myth by embracing a concept of narrative that recognizes the codeterminacy of narration and meaning. As the interlocutor notes concerning his pills, which he offers to Carmen as an aid to break her singleness of vision, "[T]hey restore [memory], but they also disorder it, something that's very pleasant" (102).

The denial of the fortuitous and, of course, disorder, prevails among historians of the Regime not only in the patterns of discourse, but also in the perception of time. Indeed, what represents temporal reciprocity and continuity for Franco becomes for Martín Gaite the embodiment of stasis. This can be seen in a variety of ways in *Cuarto*, but is most acutely visible in the metonymic identification of Franco with the flow of time. The narrator at once asserts Franco's control over time and links this control with the restraint of time as a catalyst for change. While watching Franco's burial on television, Carmen is intrigued by the appearance of Franco's daughter (whose first name Carmen shares) and by their similar experiences of Spanish culture during the past forty years. What strains against Carmen's identification with the daughter, however, is the intense awareness of time:

> And I was touched to see her walk on toward the hole in the ground in which they were going to put that man, who for her was simply her father, whereas for all other Spaniards he had been the devious and secret motive force of that block of time, the chief engineer and the inspector and the manufacturer of the transmission gears, and time itself, whose flow he had damped, damned, and directed, with the result that one barely felt either time or him move, and the imperceptible variations that inevitably came about, merely because of the passage of time, in language, in dress, in music, in human relations, in public entertainment, in places, seemed to have simply fallen from heaven. (133–34)

Martín Gaite's coupling of Franco and time thickens the meaning of the temporal focus here by bringing to the fore the central myth that shapes Franco's dominion over Spain and its past. That is to say, Franco stands as a reification of time so that what is culturally defined by the Regime appears to mark the natural flow of human progress—"the imperceptible variations that inevitably came about . . . seemed to have simply fallen from heaven." Both progress and naturalness are deeply embedded in the mythology of the Regime, of course, but as Carmen evokes the past she is able to perceive only the suspension of time as the corollary of Francoist rule: "I am simply not capable of discerning the passage of time all during that period, or differentiating the war years from the postwar ones. The thought came to me that Franco had paralyzed time, and on the very day that they were about to bury him I woke up, with my mind focused on that one thought with a very special intensity" (130).

The importance of Martín Gaite's perspective on time and history under Franco lies less with what she denounces than with the alternative conception of history that she offers in its place. She does not set out to invent new myths that dispute the old ones, but rather posits a counterdiscourse in which history is awakened to the fragmented and indeterminate essence of the subjective: "We are not just one being, but many, exactly as real history is not what is written by putting dates in their proper order and then presenting it to us as a single whole. Each person who has seen us or spoken to us at a certain time retains one piece of the puzzle that we will never be able to see all put together" (166). Thus when Martín Gaite speaks to history and contemplates a discourse of her own, she calls forth the creative authority embedded in the metaphor of her "back room":

> I must begin the book on the postwar period in a moment of sudden enlightenment like this one right now, tying together the march of history and the rhythm of dreams. It is such a vast panorama and such a topsy-turvy one, like a room where each thing is in its proper place precisely because it is out of place. All this goes back to my initial perplexities in the face of the concept of history, there in the back room, surrounded by toys and books strewn all over the floor. (98–99)

Martín Gaite clearly opens history to the reader at the level of theme in *Cuarto*, but it is the teleogenic plotting of the novel that impels her view of history beyond myth. It reveals the transformative power of individual memory to undermine the inertial monologism and fixed continuity of the past and to show instead how history is necessarily malleable. Such thinking reverses the traditional formula of first-person plotting of "Once I was lost but now I am found" and posits in its place an open-ended "I" whose discourse is epistemically fundamental to both the self and the understanding (i.e., the writing) of history.

The conception of history as the discourse of remembrance configures the opposition to myth in other postwar novels of memory as well. Luis Goytisolo's *Recuento* (1973), for example, relies heavily upon the exigencies of memory to disclose the unreliability of a single-voiced historiography. As the title suggests, Goytisolo's concern is with retelling, with renarrating the past in order to lay out the historical in an alternative frame. His story is drawn so as to criticize overtly the political dissidence and barren lives of the young bourgeoisie in postwar Spain, and the novel grows harshly sardonic as it demythifies the Spanish Left and lays bare the sterility of its dissent. But more importantly, Goytisolo vitiates the very concept of mythic historiography through his rejection of the narrative of closure.

Goytisolo's strategy is shaped in the first part of *Recuento* by his reliance upon the narrative traditions of social realism to portray bourgeois revolutionaries and their plotting against the Regime. He devotes lengthy narrative segments to the organization of the Communist party at the university and records the frequent political discussions of the student activists. Goytisolo clearly professes no sympathy for the Franco government. He confounds the image of a heroic and imperialist Spain and posits in its place a movement of dissent bound closely to the rhetorical myths of the Communist party. These myths are woven into the fabric of the novel and emerge fully at various points of the narrative to buttress the referential focus on Spain of the 1950s and 1960s. For example, the identification of the Communist party's epistemological tenets with authentic reality and truth (a crucial myth of the party's dissidence) stands clearly opposed to the Regime's positioning of itself as sole proprietor of discursive correctness:

> Look, Daniel, said Escala. What distinguishes us from any other political party, apart from differences of structural apparatus and organization, is the fact that we possess a method for analyzing reality that is completely scientific. That is to say, we are capable of appreciating reality as it truly is, with its laws and its dialectics, without allowing ourselves to be confused by events, by appearances and deceptions that can conceal reality, by things that are static or incomplete, such as trees that prevent us from seeing the forest. Obviously there may be errors of interpretation or of application, but as in any scientific field, they are subjective errors; it is the person and not the method that fails; the method is there, as objective as reality itself. (156)

But Goytisolo's aim is not to lay one set of myths (those of dissent) over and against another (those of consonance). Instead, his narrative proposition in *Recuento* (and in the whole of his tetralogy *Antagonía*) is to undermine both the myths and the mythic paradigms that hold political and narrative authority in Francoist Spain. The process for doing so is necessarily bimodal. It begins with subversion of the mythic content by means of ironic vitiation, and ends with the destruction of the mythic structure and its mechanisms of narration.

The ironic undercurrent of *Recuento* is evident throughout the novel as Goytisolo represents the activities of a group of university students whose political agenda ties them to the Communist party. These characters ape the language of revolution, organize protests and strikes against the Regime, and debate the approaching revolution in Spain in a way that, at first glance, appears to resonate with authenticity. However, their performance as dissenters proves not only to be intellectually thin, but also immensely dishonest. As Goytisolo shows, their commitment is tainted by their bourgeois desires—for wealth, for success, for attachments to power (they use the influence of their parents with the Regime to be freed from police custody)—and by a debilitating inertia. As one member of the group observes, "lamentably, the intellectual who becomes a revolutionary is frequently motivated by dark animosities, by idealized thinking, behind which frequently there is hidden a hypocritical and antisocial personality, one that is definitely sick" (213).

The irony is more intensely destructive, however, when the dissidents embrace the very mythic structures used by the Regime to set forth the Communist perspective on history. Francoist historiography in general, as we have seen, identifies a sanctioned register of heroes (el Cid, Isabel la Católica, Felipe II, etc.) to serve as precursors to the heroic lineage of the Regime. Ironically, the group of student activists co-opts the rhetorical mythmaking of the state in order to couple its own program to a legitimating past. The following passage merits quoting at length, since it reveals fully the Party's ironic reversal of Francoist mythology and the meanings attached to it by the Regime:

> It is possible to interpret the Spanish Civil War correctly only by inserting it into the general struggle of the Spanish people for their freedom, since to say Ebro or Jarama is like saying Bailén or Bruchs, and countless other heroic battles by our people, the people who invented revolutionary struggle *par excellence*, guerrilla warfare, to

combat the Napoleonic invaders. Furthermore, taking into account Franco's use of Moorish mercenaries, it is relevant to establish a relationship of continuity even with the Reconquest, with the eight centuries of struggle that the Hispanic people sustained against Arabic expansionism, Roncesvalles, the Navas de Tolosa, Mallorca, Sevilla, Valencia, and Granada, landmarks of our history that perhaps the eternal enemies of Spain, those crafty foes who are anti-Spain, prefer to overlook. In other words: our achievement can and ought to be placed in the line of great national achievements, of those singular undertakings whose symbols are the Cid, Isabel the Catholic, Don Quijote, Cortés, Pizarro, and so many other heroes whose deeds our people have celebrated for centuries and centuries and which, either in chronicles or through oral tradition, have passed from generation to generation and which, also from generation to generation, our people have reinvigorated with new contributions from their own blood, the glorious Crusade of Liberation being the most recent and no less important than those of yesteryear. . . . (525–26)

In the context of the given history of Spain (i.e., the history of the Regime), this passage evokes for the reader the Communist party's view of the Civil War as a glorious crusade for freedom. The war is tied to previous conflicts in which Spain fought for the ideas of liberty, as well as to the larger body of traits of an essential Spain which were reified by the Reconquista, sanctified by the Catholic sovereigns, and carried to a distant continent by Cortés and Pizarro. These myths, along with the rhetorical paradigms that embody them, are mirror images of those propagated by the Regime, but they now bear new, antithetical meanings. At first glance, this opposition suggests that Goytisolo, though critical of the shallow rhetoric of the Communist party, embraces the larger message of defiance that it conveys. In other words, he condemns the dictatorship and sides with the dissidents. The concern that lies at the heart of Goytisolo's novel, however, is not that one political group or another is able to provide a "correct" meaning of history, but that the historiographic paradigm formulated by both is based on facile assumptions about the nature of narration and the way of understanding the past. To see how this is so, it is necessary to draw forth the contingencies of both knowing and narrating in Goytisolo's scheme, as he forcefully subverts the very structure upon which the myths of Spanish history have been constructed. He does so through the mediation of Raúl, who seeks a personal identity within a narrative of memory that reverses the spiraling energy of mythic discourse toward closure and stasis.

The hermeneutics of writing in Goytisolo's novel claims historical authenticity not by the proclaimed objectivity of the referential illusion, but by the insertion of a self (Raúl) into the telling of a story that has the fixed structures of mythic discourse as its implied referent. The narrative moves from the traditional perspective of third-person omniscience early in the novel to more stylistically and technically intricate machinations in the latter chapters as the "retelling" of the past grows ever more personal and subjective. The long and complex sequence on the history of Cataluña and Spain at the end of chapter 7 (277–91) illustrates the intensity of the subjective within a discourse whose subject is history. The narrator first proposes "an intricate history" (278), and then proceeds to lay out how such a history may be opened to diversity and dissent: "the task of constructing a Spain that is different in terms of its voluntary unity in socialism, unity without uniformity, unity in diversity, decentralization compatible with democratic centralism, revolutionary nationalism understood as opposition to the capitalist world . . . " (290). What emerges from the lengthy sequence that brackets the historical here points to the two important levels of the novel that stand opposed to social realism: (1) the way in which history, still the referent of the narrative, is demythified through the drawing forth of a range of dialectical propositions; (2) the mediation of history by a subjective voice whose very subjectivity implies a hermeneutics based not on "being there" (i.e., the testimonial objectivity of social realism), but on narration and memory—history that is "true" not because it inheres in an abstract or found discourse outside the text, but because it is tied to a subjective life that is always bound up with the past, with history. This "withinness" supersedes "being there" in the novels of memory and reveals how history (and historiography) must always be redeemed outside the static structures of myth and within the discernment of a narrating self. The double redemption of history and the self is embodied through the evocation of an individual past and, as

Proust put it, "the joy of rediscovering what is real" (3: 913). Proust's discovery of the real hinges, of course, on the way in which the self and history open the contingencies of their truths to one another and on the way in which these contingencies are narrated.

Thus when Raúl contemplates his writing in relation to the past (both his self and events outside of his self) he rejects "the heroic prose of his militant period" (626), that is to say, the prose of a single-voiced discourse. He rejects as well the myth of his own being as it has been defined by his oxymoronic attachment to the bourgeois Communist party. He has traversed the present and past both of Spain and his own family only to forswear them, and now the burden of giving meaning to his life turns upon the perception of a reinvigorated self within time and history. Raúl does not seek to be liberated from the past, but from the narrow straits of its inuring control. Hence as he leaps into the unknown he calls forth the formative authority of narration. He recognizes the risk that discourse may congeal into a solidified mass of repetitive musings ("And thus it is, from the time that in earliest infancy one establishes a specific system of relations between names and things, one excludes the possibility of any other system of relations" [621–22]), and thus denounces the narrative traditions of social realism which promote univocal meanings: "You can't write a novel about us, which in fact is what his [Adolfo's] novel is, a roman à clé, which is limited to observations of a part of our behavior without penetrating beyond the surface, without giving [that behavior] at least some meaning—whatever it may be—that makes it literarily valid" (348). He opts finally for the creative dispersion of subjective narration over the sterile imposition of the referential illusion. Raúl does not propose solipsism, but rather embraces the enabling energy of words to free him from the black opacity of myth. He thus combats the implicit agenda of myth through which change bears no meaning and meaning can undergo no change. This is explicitly laid out by the insinuation of the "I" (Raúl) into a long chain of historical events:

> Then in the same way that it is difficult to discern if it is frightful to consider, for example, the influence over a person of facts so distant in time and space such as the founding of Rome, the formation of Barcino in the womb of the future Roman Empire, its Chris-

tianization following the arrival of Santiago, its reconquest by Wilfred the Hairy, the reception of honor given to Columbus by the city after his return from the discovery, the departure for America by a Ferrer who made a fortune there and who joined up with a Gaminde, the return to the peninsula of a branch of the family . . . the wedding of their son Jorge with Eulalia Moret, the birth of Raúl, the war . . . military service, the Party, Leo and Federico, the Model Jail, *I, here at this moment, or on the contrary, such a chain doesn't exist, that the alternative of a contingent fact can only be another contingent fact, the absolute domain of the arbitrary.* (616, emphasis mine)

Nothing can be preserved for the present without being altered, and Raúl's insistence on the "the absolute domain of the arbitrary" confirms not only his own indeterminacy in history, but that of his discourse as it lays bare the aporias of being in time. The meaning of the past (and present) is therefore not "given" within a perceived natural flow of events (as asserted by historians of the Regime), but rather is wholly constructed. This construction takes place within the crucible of the self (which is always in time) and is projected into the world through the epiphany of narration: "The golden moment, the feeling that through the written word he was not only creating something autonomous, alive, but that in the course of this process of objectivization through writing he was able at once to understand the world through himself and to know himself through the world" (623). In this way Raúl becomes master of time and meaning rather than their servant, and thereby subverts the sacred esthetics of the State.

Another important way in which the "withinness" of the remembering character shapes the narration of history pertains closely to the use of texts. Narrators who consistently evoke the past in the first person most often give their historical accounts the generic feeling of a memoir. First-person narration generally provokes anxiety over matters of truth, less because a narrowed perspective suggests overt unreliability (though this may indeed be the case, as in a novel such as Luis Goytisolo's *La cólera de Aquiles*) than because of the special pleadings inherent in a highly personalized discourse on the past and the associative uncertainties of memory. In order to diminish the imputation of unreliability in their treatment of the historical (and conversely, in order to enhance the authenticity of their perspective), narrators of memory often insert a wide variety of texts into their discourse: news items, reports, photographic albums, maps, portraits, and the like. These texts appear in narrated form, of course (with the exception of Juan Benet's cartographic images), and bear upon two issues that directly confront all first-person discourse: (1) the preoccupation with not only asserting that something has occurred, but with the disclosure of corroborative evidence that buttresses the remembering narrator's evocation of it; (2) the fundamental role of interpretation in the discernment not of the truth, but of the meaning of discourse. While the historiographic impact of social realism stems largely from the way it collapses truth and meaning into a structure that seeks to close itself to interpretation (i.e., the truth is evident and available for all to see), the novelists of memory imply several possible answers and, more importantly, intimate that each text engenders several possible questions. In this sense the narrative not only states and asserts, but it also possesses a horizon of unasserted possibilities of meaning (i.e., propositions) that lie beyond intention and beyond myth.

For example, Juan Goytisolo's *Señas de identidad* (1966) contains texts both as a sign of the real and as a mechanism for foregrounding the operations of interpreting. Alvaro Mendiola's reliance upon photos, postcards, letters, maps, and other documents to piece together the past (both his own and that of Spain) reveals the reciprocity between history as a formative component of the self and the self as a formative component of history. The texts validate the "realness" of the past (people, places, events actually exist), but the meaning of this past has yet to be determined. What is crucial about the determination of meaning here (and in other novels of memory as well) is that Alvaro does not set out to reconstruct the past as past, as if it existed as an isolated whole within its own structure of meaning. Instead he draws upon texts as framers of experience and integrates them into his own thoughts, desires, and needs in the present. Rather than stand apart from all that surrounds him and precedes him, Alvaro is firmly attached to history; he is *in* history. As Joel Weinsheimer writes, summarizing Gadamer, "Our present, our difference from the past, is not the obstacle but the very condition of understanding the past . . . and the past to which we have access is always our own past by reason of our belonging to it" (134). The history that Alvaro is in, of course, only is knowable through his narration of it, laid out by the multitude of telescopic relations among the events, photos, and documents of the past. The texts themselves stand inert and lifeless until they are awakened to meaning by memory and narration. Indeed, as Alvaro contemplates the past during the course of the novel, he is struck by the necessity of his role as narrator of that past: "If you are dead (you said to yourself) upon whom will it fall to tell it [the past]?" (230); "his rebelliousness against Spanish society of his time died with him [his uncle] as no doubt yours will die with you if you don't give it a concrete and precise form if you don't manage to give it shape" (346); "You knew that, upon your death, the past would be annihilated with you. It depended upon you, solely upon you, to save it from disaster" (156). History is thus set forth as a component of narration, sustained here by the view that Alvaro is permanently bound up with the complementary need for historical and self-definition.

Goytisolo constantly moves the definition of self between past and present as his character erupts into the epiphany of knowing. Again, the role of texts is preeminent. Similar to Luis Goytisolo in *Recuento*, Juan Goytisolo in *Señas* subverts the traditions of social realism as both a literary form and as a way of representing life. For example, in the midst of a segment in which the narrative embodies the empty rhetoric of dissent of Spanish exiles in Paris (a rhetoric closely affiliated with that of the Communist party portrayed in *Recuento*), the narrator alludes to a magazine founded by the group (though never published) and relates the materials listed in the table of contents. Among other things, the issue was to have included "a dull essay . . . in defense of realism, a leaden, roundtable discussion on the commitment of writers" (257). Goytisolo then offers a sample of "committed poetry" (258) written by an opponent of the Franco regime. What is important to understand here is that, ironically, the poem itself (i.e., its rhetoric) is the object of Goytisolo's scorn rather than the regime against which the poem speaks. The poem is placed amid the empty rhetoric of dissent mouthed by the exiles in Madame Berger's café—a contrived rhetoric of mythic pretension which, as Goytisolo shows, has futilely sought to bring about social and political change in Spain. The interpolation of the poem at this point underscores the likeness between the two types of rhetoric—of the poem and the exiles—rather than affirm their difference. It thereby denigrates the explicit literary intent of the poem and reveals the vacuity of its social substance.

More importantly, however, the poem is linked to the same kind of mythic discourse used by the Regime to co-opt reality and give it a narrow set of meanings. The mechanical patterns of expression in the poem are denotative and sterile (as are those of the Franco regime) rather than ambiguous and complex. To engender authentic changes in the perceptions of Spanish reality (both past and present), the writer must vitiate the prevailing linguistic presuppositions of the Regime.[4] These are not only insipid and stale, but they represent a fixed archaism that serves to legitimate the language of political power used by the State. Further, as Jonathan Morse has shown, the use of this kind of language "assures those who hear the old words that their history is in safe hands" (3). The language of social realism uses the very language of the Regime in an attempt to disrupt the mythic structures of control. However, it serves only to reinforce the status quo at the level of narration and therefore, in Goytisolo's view, must be destroyed and refashioned in a new mold. Alvaro's evocation of the past, and his urgency to narrate, adumbrate not simply one more form of representational fiction, but rather lay out an antimythic narration that cuts at the very heart of Francoist rhetoric.

This idea is more directly related to past time in the final chapter of *Señas*, where fragments of conversations among tourists are juxtaposed to a government pamphlet outlining the history of Barcelona. As Alvaro, now beyond memory in the pure present, concurrently listens to fragments of conversations in foreign languages and reads a tourist pamphlet outlining the history of the city, he absorbs the full extent to which the Regime has appropriated the past and made it the enterprise of the State. Alvaro disdains the foreign words of the tourists with the same contempt that he views the new buildings of Barcelona—each in its own way has strangled the city and effaced its identity. Most importantly, however, because the pamphlet is framed within the narrative by the persistent alienation that informs Alvaro's memory, it reveals how narration is used by the government to abridge culture and rid it of its complexity and richness. The official discourse of the Regime (the syncopating function of which has already been established in *Señas* by the intercalated texts of the press and the police) is now exposed in the whole of its sterility as antithetical to truth. It reveals less about the past of Barcelona—as is its intention—than about the reductivist efficiency and mythifying power of narration when appropriated by the government to serve the aim of historical continuity and orthodoxy.

Narrated texts also inform the historiographic concerns of *El cuarto de atrás*. The novel is overrun by a number of texts (e.g., the "novela rosa," letters, detective fiction, poetry, songs, film, a book on insanity, and paintings, among others), but is overtly shaped by Todorov's view of the fantastic. *Cuarto* as the embodiment of a fantastic novel, and *Cuarto* about the writing of a fantastic novel, are of course central to the meaning of the work, as critical commentary has frequently pointed out (see, for example, the books on Martín Gaite by Joan Brown and by Mirella Servodidio and Marcia Welles). But what is most pertinent here is the way in which text, memory, and history are balanced on the fulcrum of interpretation to convey how history is always provisional. Martín Gaite explicitly sets *Cuarto* over and against the texts of social realism as a mode of writing, but does not deny her novel a social agenda. The social in this case coincides intimately with historiography and the appropriations of the past under Franco, as well as with the way in which the past is made known. From the cult of Isabel la Católica and the myth of "the perfect Spanish woman" (96) to the recurrent image of Carmencita Franco (with songs of the 1940s and the TV news interspersed prominently), *Cuarto* affirms how interpretation of the past is always ongoing, always contingent upon memory, even when a text offers compelling evidence of truth. Memory forgets, revises, and transforms so that the past remains ever open to rewriting and reinterpreting in ways that defy the design of myth. The texts that Martín Gaite infiltrates in *Cuarto* are both in history (they possess the "reality" of existing outside her novel) and about history—they were used by the Regime to tell its version of the truth. These texts are renarratized within the frame of memory, and what is recovered is time itself. As Martín Gaite writes, "How much time wasted, how many useless wanderings back and forth through this apartment, down through the years, searching for something. What am I searching for now? Ah, yes, the track of time. As always, time is what gets lost most often" (25). The reconciliation that occurs between a past once closed to interpretation and a memory with full desire to interpret, recaptures history as subjective meaning engendered to annul myth. In short, nothing is preserved for Martín Gaite, nothing is remembered and given meaning, without being altered.

Luis Goytisolo's *La cólera de Aquiles* (1979) speaks even more explicitly to the textual foundation of memory and narration and the contingencies of writing history. The historical referent in this case (the same anti-Francoist militants living in Paris that Juan Goytisolo portrays in *Señas de identidad*) is shown not only open to the changing paradigms of narration but also to the creative interpretation of the reader. Matilde Moret's intercalated short novel, *El edicto de Milán*, recounts Matilde's experiences with Spanish exiles in Paris, but as her narrative develops it offers varied and conflicting perspectives on the same set of incidents. The novel can thus be seen as doubly contestatory: it directly subverts the myth of its own context (i.e., the framing narration of Aquiles which, ironically, is portrayed in the novel through a painting [a text] that may be purely fictitious); and it destabilizes a single-voiced discourse that asserts truths about the past (Matilde's recollections of anti-Francoist activities among the students). The novel lays open to doubt the mythical wrath of Aquiles (236, 239), but more importantly, it challenges all narrative that pretends to assert truths rather than propose meanings. The demythification of the Spanish intellectual Left is deeply embedded in *Cólera*, but the novel offers no alternative myth in its place. Instead, the focus shuttles back and forth between the writing and reading of texts, and reveals how both activities are bound up with our understanding of the past.

This is especially the case in *Cólera* with the act of reading. The novel consists of Matilde reading the novel that we are reading (*Cólera*), as well as her rereading of *El edicto de Milán*, the novel that she wrote some years before. Both novels are built upon contradictions purposely forged by the author (Matilde), and thus loosen the hold of univocal meanings and congealed truths—in this case, truth concerning the bourgeois Spanish exiles and Matilde herself. But the shift in emphasis from writer to reader in *Cólera* represents as well a reconsignment of sense-giving in the narrative process. While it is true that this process is bound up with the text and its author/narrator, Goytisolo insists that it is equally attached to self-creation of the individual reader. Similar to Juan Goytisolo in *Señas*, Goytisolo represents Spanish exiles in *Cólera* to set forth a mythic discourse of dissent. Additionally, as occurs in *Señas*, he casts this dissent within the frame of ridicule and irony, thus denigrating both it and those who zealously pronounce it. He does so not by laying alongside this discourse a particular counterdiscourse with a more cogent or coherent message, but rather by placing the meaning of the rhetoric of dissent in the hands of a remembering reader. The novel *La cólera de Aquiles*, while wholly metafictional in the way that it exposes the material of its own composition, has much to assert as well about the importance and nature of its reception:

> The foolish part of theories of information, therefore, is that they leave out precisely what ought to be their focus, which is reading. Not the text, but the reading of the text. Not the content itself of the message, but the reading of that message. Not the form in which it appears, but the impact that it causes. Not the bullet, but the shot. (296)

As Robert Spires has suggested, *Cólera* forms part of a group of texts that "read themselves into existence" (*Metafictional* 106). In the context of knowing the past, this focus undermines the authority not only of those who generate discourse, but also of those who attribute specific meanings to it. The creative authority granted the reader enables the individual self to be integrated into the full circulation of meaning ("[reading is] an experience as revealing, sometimes, as that of writing" [316]), and also dismisses the closure of myth in favor of subjectivity and openness: "Every reading, from that of the master work to the latest comic, establishes subject matter that each reader reshapes according to a particular viewpoint" (295).

It must be pointed out, however, that Goytisolo does not seek to affirm the value of reading over writing as a source of truth. Rather, he locates the meaning of discourse on the threshold of contingency. The entire creative process, therefore, is tied intimately to the inventing of texts and the creation of a self: "In works of fiction, in much greater measure than in testimonial or speculative texts, the reader discovers in the world things until then unimagined that offer him an immediate knowledge of the world as well as of himself" (239). Fiction is superior to history here (and implicitly to myth), not because of the truth value of its discourse but because of its propositions about truth. The epistemological fabric of narration implies always the hand of the weaver, which in turn affirms the presence of a self through which meaning (and in this case, the historical meaning of intellectual dissidence) is mediated and engendered. It is in this sense that history is afforded its most diverse and profound possibilities in the novel of memory. As with Ricoeur, "the meaning of history resides in its aspect as a drama of the human effort to endow life with meaning" (White, *Content* 181). Time is always corrosive, and memory can recoup never time itself but only the meaning of time for a remembering self. This is what the novelists of memory propose at every turn of their writing, and what places their narrative in opposition to the assertive truths of social realism and historiography under Franco.

For the novelists of memory, as I have sought to show, the writing of history cannot be collapsed into the reductivist and debilitating paradigm of myth. Indeed, in the major lineage of fiction in Spain from the mid-1960s to the present (e.g., Benet, Juan Goytisolo, Luis Goytisolo, Martín Gaite, some of the work of Cela and Delibes), memory serves to sap the roots of myth-producing narrations and to shed the thick wrapping of narrative closure. To evoke the historical past for these novelists is conceived not as experiencing that past as it once might have been lived, but as filtering time through the consciousness of a remembering self at once in history and open to history. Time for the novelists of memory is thus not a chasm that is merely bridged for the recovery of the historical. It is rather, as Gadamer writes, "a ground which supports the arrival of the past and where the present takes its roots" ("Problem" 152). This interplay (or dialogue, as some would have it) between present and past defines the narrating selves of these works and their discourse on history. In contrast to social realism and the historiography of the State, therefore, the novel of memory lays out history as a series of disruptions—of time, of self, of narration, and most importantly, of the referential illusion of truth and wholeness.

The remembering discoursers in the novels that I have discussed are most often alienated and adrift in postwar Spain—in part because they bear the full weight of the past, in part because they know that this weight can be grasped as something meaningful that has nothing immutable about it except that it can never be defined once and for all. To respect the wholeness of the past means to leave it open to inquiry, to refuse to neutralize the contingencies of history by transforming them into the safe zone of myth. Indeed, the novel of memory works consistently to decenter the paradigm of myth and to reconstitute the center as a moveable construct that always questions the past and remains open to the hermeneutics of dissent.

4

Narrative Enigmas:

History and Fiction in Juan Benet

There are more things in heaven and earth, Horatio,

Than are dreamt of in your philosophy.

—William Shakespeare, *Hamlet*, Act I

As we have seen to this point, the hermeneutic arch linking fiction to history in Francoist Spain undermines both naive and doctrinaire meanings attributed to the past. In the works of social realism it turns one declared truth (the truth of myth) against another, while in the novel of memory it gives to history a protean mutability rooted in the aporias of time. In the novels and essays of Juan Benet, the filiation of history and fiction is refined and extended, but at the same time it gains a kind of liquefying amorphousness. I do not mean this in a negative sense—that Benet stands radically apart from literary and historical traditions in postwar Spain in his understanding of the past, or that his writing is abusively remote and inaccessible (though, to be sure, it is supremely difficult). Amorphousness here refers to a recurrent intentionality in Benet's writing to fuse opposing horizons and contradictory shapes so that his work becomes a rich admixture of referential illusion and enigmatic contingency, always malleable (but never chaotic) as it reaches into the deepest folds of historical inquiry. In Benet's writing there is little that might be perceived as a propositional system or a conceptual rigidity offering specific judgments about one historiographic method or another. But more than any other novelist of postwar Spain Benet reveals in his work a primary concern both with history and the writing of history.[1] This intentionality can be discerned in nearly all of his fiction, and is enunciated as well in a number of essays that define his historiographic thinking.

Benet demonstrates in his work an awareness not only of the problems of historical writing in general, but of Francoist historiography in particular during the 1940s and 1950s. Benet of course was a university student during the first decade following the Civil War and, like others of his generation, studied history within the narrow interpretive frame laid out by historians of the Regime. But such a frame, Benet knew, served only to prop up those who had constructed it and permitted little opportunity to break from given paradigms or to explore new perspectives. In his essay "Sobre el carácter tétrico de la historia" (1970), for example, Benet assails the teaching of history in the context of Francoism:

> What is not acceptable is to teach history with a specific tone, be it nationalist, religious, or cultural, because that is a far cry from what history is. . . . The history that a child studies is, as a rule, a series of inaccuracies, a false story that compels him to grow old with an incorrect view of many essential things: of his own time, of the time of his parents, of his country, his religion, and his culture. (*Puerta* 177–78)

Part of Benet's criticism stems from his view of historiography in general—a reticence, as we shall see, to endow any discourse whose project is past time with an imperious claim to truth. But his concerns are also rooted in his own circumstances of postwar Spain and the imposed homogeneity of historical understanding, neatly summed up in the Regime's synoptic slogan, "We are at peace."

Adam Schaff has pointed out that in times of quiescence (even when this quiescence is imposed, such as during the Franco regime), historians frequently emphasize the tranquillity of the past so as not to disrupt the present. In contrast, in periods of stress (the perception of Spain held by the declared opponents of the Regime), those who are dissatisfied with the present are likely to draw forth dissonance in their representation of the past. At such times, as Carl Becker puts it, "historians . . . will be disposed to cross-examine the past . . . to sit in judgment on what was formerly done, approving or disapproving in the light of present discontents" (*Essays* 169–70). Benet voices a similar perspective on how the present plays a role in determining the past, and he links dissatisfaction with dissidence: "I suspect that historical interpretations—above all those written out of need—come to light only in periods of political malaise; they respond to the question of the doctor who, in order to outline the clinical history of his patient, expresses interest in the illnesses he has suffered. When people are in good health they don't care about measles. The hermeneutics [of history] therefore is usually more indicative of the patient's current state of health than of his past health" ("De nuevo" 12). Any hint of "political malaise" is of course disaffirmed by the Regime, and the "patient" (Spain) is judged to be in fine health. In his fiction Benet draws explicitly upon the diseased body metaphor to characterize postwar Spain, but in his essays (and in the context of teaching) he merely laments the pedagogical calamity of history. As he writes in *Puerta de tierra*, "[Regulated teaching] may be justified in some powerful countries, but even those in the clearest and most open decline—let us take Spain as an example—take great care to avoid confessing such a state of affairs, and are careful, apparently, to convince students of the good fortune they have had to be born in such a favored part of the world" (179).

But it is not the reception of history by students that ultimately interests Benet. Rather he is concerned with how the writing of history is shaped and sustained as a form of intellectual inquiry and how it serves the human need to understand not only the past, but to take the measure of future horizons as well. In his immediate circumstances, of course, Benet must confront the deficiencies of historiography in postwar Spain. On the most elementary level, this means simply having access to information. But here, as occurs with the thornier problems of truth and meaning, the State exerts autocratic control. In his review of José Manuel Martínez Bande's book, *La marcha sobre Madrid*, for example, Benet condemns the withholding of crucial archival information on the military aspects of the Civil War. He observes that the "facts" of the war, which are contained in the files of what the government calls the

"Archives of the War of Liberation," remain closed to scholars who do not parrot the official posture of the Regime ("'La marcha'" 60–61). As a result, opposition writers who have attempted to research the war must often rely upon memoirs and personal testimony, and therefore can offer few facts to buttress arguments that controvert the assertions of the Regime.

Benet also denounces the arid simplicity that shapes the historiography of the State. For example, when Américo Castro's *España en su historia* (1948) was rereleased in its original form in 1983, Benet reflected upon the essentialist intentions of historians in the 1940s and the way in which they sought an ur-explanation for the decline of Spain before the country was saved by the Francoist Crusade: "For some, the problem stems from the weakness of Castilian-Aragonese feudalism; others will point to the lack of a true Renaissance; others will undoubtedly suggest the absence of a reform movement; later will come the lack of an Enlightenment, of an industrial revolution, of a commitment to Europe, and so on up to the present time" ("De nuevo" 11). The absence of "a vital element, essential for [Spain's] unity and progress" (11) allowed historians of the Regime to explain Spanish decay in Orteguian terms and to co-opt certain moments of the past as the embodiment of a mythic truth. Thus, for example, the linking of Francoism to a previous era (the Middle Ages) when a "vital element" emanated from Christianity. In his consideration of such matters of the past in his own work, Benet of course has absorbed these fundamental propositions of Francoist historiography, but he renounces both their form and substance at every turn.

In most of his writing on history Benet is less concerned with the specific components of Francoist historiography than with the general principles that embody the historiographic enterprise as a whole. Most importantly, Benet seeks to locate the writing of history in the larger field of narration. For example, in *La inspiración y el estilo* (1965), one of his early books on writing, Benet subordinates the exclusionary domain of what might be termed the "historian's history" to the wider notion of history that explicitly includes the novel: "The meaning of the word 'history' can be as broad as one wishes to make it, as long as it includes everything written with the goal of awakening interest in specific facts; in our time it would also have to include almost the entire field of the novel and the majority of those narratives that are still called 'stories' ['historias']" (166). While history and fiction seem to coalesce here under the larger domain of "story," and while indeed it is Benet's intention to scumble the boundaries that have sustained the discreteness of the two fields, their merger in this instance is not as seamless as it appears. The obstacle that quickly surfaces in Benet's thinking, and which runs throughout his writing to underscore generic difference, is the presence of *facts*. Despite Nietzsche's well-known declaration of the death of fact and the rule of interpretation, Benet not only attaches traditional historical significance to facts, but appears to endow them with a verifiable truth value. He by no means stands alone in taking such a position. In addition to the large body of science-based historians of our time, metahistorical theorists such as Paul Ricoeur and Hayden White have also asserted the centrality of facts to the writing of history. Ricoeur maintains, for example, that the historian's use of documents and other factual materials creates a line of division between history and fiction (*Time* 3: 142), and White, even while affirming the narrational base of historical writing, acknowledges the usefulness of historical facts that exist *in reality*, outside of narration (*Content* ch. 7).

For Benet, although the meaning of facts grows from the story in which they are emplotted, their existence (the realness of their existence) precedes essence. For example, in *La inspiración y el estilo* Benet discusses in historical writing "facts about which there is not the least bit of uncertainty" (52). He observes that, in contrast to the poet, "the historian still has an interest in facts" (168), and he further sets forth the "dictate of facts" (168) that shapes the work of the historian. In his history of the Civil War, *¿Qué fue la guerra civil?*, Benet frequently alludes to facts in order to give legitimacy to one point or another. For example, he offers "proven facts" (15) to show that the Republican government had no role in the assassination of José Calvo Sotelo in July of 1936. When depicting the violent atmosphere of that year, he shows that "[when] the facts become so compelling, both sides end up being equally responsible" (15); or when he discusses the length of the war, he affirms that, "It has been clearly proven that the officers who rebelled did not want an armistice" (78). I use these examples not to point specifically to aspects of the Civil War that Benet finds significant, but to show that he believes in an objective reality that exists in time (history) and that is available to the cognitive processes of the historian. Historical facts are of course the consequence of acts of research, information gathered from material made available to the researcher. In this sense, Benet's commitment to facts has a strong political impetus as well as a philosophical one—in the context of Francoist Spain the (in)ability of historians to get at the facts became nearly as important as the facts themselves.

Yet as most readers of Benet know, his is a world constructed and sustained not by the rigid adherence to one reality or another, but by the enriching openness of contradiction and uncertainty.[2] This holds true for nearly all of his fiction, but equally important, emerges as a formative and epistemological principle of his theoretical writing as well. Hence there is an opposing proposition in Benet's essays on history, one that overtly gives historical facts a diminished significance. This proposition takes root in a relativist perception of the past and is tied to the historiographic concept of presentism. Within this context, the facts of history, differentiated from the imagined events of fiction, come to represent for Benet a peripheral component of his historiographic project. In the end, it is the art of narration for Benet that enables the writer to probe more deeply into the past and that allows fiction and history to share temporal explorations.

While positivist historians embrace objective reflection and representation as disciplinary requisites, presentist historians (often identified with relativists and used synonymously) negate the very notion of an objective historical process.[3] In its place they posit history as the function of circumstantial interests and needs. As Schaff writes, drawing upon Carl Becker, "The principal idea rests in the conviction that an historian should be allotted the 'freedom of a creative artist'; that in writing history he, of necessity, presents a mixture of facts and fantasies; in a word, that history is, in one way or another, a subjective product conditioned by the specific present of the historian" (95). Since what appears in our histories is selected by the historian, and since the historian operates in a present time that is removed from the past, history is always relative, always dependent on the present for both its truth and meaning. Such thinking tends to negate distinctions between the events (viewed as facts) of history and the telling (narrating) of history, and offers instead the adumbration of a conceptual collapse.

History becomes the writing of history, and the historian, as cognizing subject, constitutes a part of that history.

At first glance, the relativistic/presentist conception of history seems foreign to Benet's insistence on getting at the facts of the matter. Indeed, whether facts are placed in a chronological temporal scheme or a fragmented one, or whether they are incorporated into a narrative perspective rooted in the present or the past, their essential "objectness" remains the same (what we might term the truth of occurrence). But it is clear that Benet does not feel at ease leaving the matter here— positivism not only simplifies a process that is acutely complex and varied, but also eliminates the contingency of meaning inherent in the two formative elements of historiography: time and narration. Thus while the intrinsic character of the facts may remain unaltered within variable and even conflicting narrative and temporal schemes, the role these facts assume in our real-life judgments about them is highly unstable (what we might term the contingent nature of the truth of meaning). In other words, time and language must be accounted for in metahistorical ways before historical meaning can be defined and legitimated.

For Benet, this means beginning at the very beginning: "[Time is] an ordering of elements before which these elements existed in Chaos" (*En ciernes* 106). Chaos is overcome and time ordered not simply through cognition (i.e., our awareness of being in time), but through the primary agency of language: "Time began with the organization of language and therefore that crazed apostle John was not all that misguided when he affirmed that in the beginning was the word" (*En ciernes* 107); "It is not at all strange that the realm of absolute time in man's life has gained a pivotal role in linguistic constructs" (*Angel* 138). In other words, we are not only fully immersed in time (and therefore in history) as human beings who dwell in this world, but we have invented a symbolic system that enables us to attach meaning to time as it affects our lives (i.e., our awareness of being in history).

There is certainly nothing radical in Benet's assertion that time and language are crucial aspects of how we understand history. Common sense dictates such a posture, even within the most obscure metahistorical considerations. What gives depth to Benet's perception of history, and what enables it to contravene the historiography of the Regime, turns upon his particular view of time within history, and how narration necessarily carries the writer (and reader) beyond fact and beyond myth. When Benet writes, for example, that "the narrator, before everything, and above all, depends upon the axis of time to establish the nature of his discourse" (*En ciernes* 16), he advances a double proposition: (1) that time and order depend upon the discursive function of language; (2) that time itself (as Ricoeur has shown) is the ultimate referent of human discourse. Narration for Benet creates not just tales *of* time (as Ricoeur points out, "structural transformations that affect situations and characters take time" [*Time* 2: 101]) but also tales *about* time. And not merely any aspect of time (chronological, subjective, etc.), but temporal aporias. As White notes (discussing Ricoeur), these aporias must be spoken about in the idiom of symbolic discourse (rather than in logical and technical discourse) and, most importantly, they "cannot be spoken about directly without contradiction" (*Content* 175).

The concept of contradiction, central to both White and Ricoeur, resonates with equal force in Benet's writing on the nature of narration and history. The essential pursuit of narration, as Benet has often averred, is exploration of the "zone of shadows." This does not mean that Benet eschews the rational, the facts of existence as we are able to know them. On the contrary, as I have shown, he embraces them as an integral component of historical knowledge. What it does bring to the fore, however, is Benet's view of history, coincident with his perception of time, in which enigma becomes the deep meaning explored by the writer and where the exploration itself (i.e., discourse as ontological) is paramount: "More important than the attempt to limit and resolve, when possible, the numerous enigmas of nature, society, man, and history—the functions of which correspond wholly to the sciences—[literature] desires to present enigmas, preserve them, conserve them in their unfathomable obscurity, demonstrate their epistemological inadequacy and their insolubility" (*En ciernes* 48–49). In other words, the symbolic discourse of narration veers from the space of science (the factual / positivistic) and enters, in Benet's words, a shadowy zone of uncertainty. This zone is constituted by "antiscience" (*En ciernes* 50) and it compels the narrator to weigh how "the sphere illuminated by science is surrounded by a dark space so extensive that the pretension to limit existence to the realm of knowledge seems ridiculous" (*En ciernes* 51).

But it is not just a matter of moving from one zone (certainty, logic, reason) to another (ambiguity, enigma, mystery), as if changing from one set of clothes to another. The lines of demarcation between zones are blurred, and as one zone penetrates the other, meaning and truth are collapsed into "the open space between affirmation and its corresponding negation" (*En ciernes* 52). At precisely this juncture Benet lays bare the heart of his theory, for within this open space we encounter "a terrain where all mode of certainty is chimerical, questionable, and sterile: where the boundaries of rationality and irrationality have no relevance and where—thanks to the aperture introduced by contradiction and mystery—the spirit of conflict between opposites predominates. It is the domain of oxymoron: only the fleeting endures and remains, everything true reveals its falseness, everything obvious contains a mystery" (*En ciernes* 53). And as Benet underscores throughout his writing, the "domain of oxymoron" contains within it the full spectrum of enigmas of what we call history.

Benet's emphasis on the oxymoronic and the contradictory as it shapes our ability both to know and to narrate the past gains particular importance in the context of postwar Spain. Above all, it shakes the foundational solidity of Francoist historiography in the way that it rejects narrative certainties: the rigidity of myth set forth by the Regime is superseded in Benet's conceptual frame by the demands of ambiguity. Equally important, however, Benet's insistence upon the contradictory nature of temporal and narrative explorations gives a protean essentialism (an oxymoronic posture in itself) to his thinking that precludes ascribing a single and unchangeable meaning to the past. In this way, the parameters of historiography for Benet become malleable and form a crucial part of a historicist perspective that undermines at every point the rigid assertions of the Regime.

Benet's historicism is born from the open spaces of paradox and contradiction and from his rejection of temporal and narrational perspectives that propound fixed laws of human existence.[4] His intention to pursue historical meaning "beyond all dogmas" (*En ciernes* 23) at once sets him squarely opposed to the end of history proposed by the Regime and opens the way for a more dynamic perception of historical writing. The concept of historicism thus becomes critical both to Benet's fiction and theory, above all for its resolute resistance to certitude and closure. As Adam Schaff has shown, the historicist perspective "is opposed to all theories proclaiming absolute values (in particular moral ones), absolute appraisals (in particular aesthetic), absolute norms (in particular ethical)" (159). Within this context, Benet's view of time and narration creates multiple senses which strain against the static truths derived from myth. The open field of historical truth for Benet thus obtains through the variable juxtapositions of contingent truths, now perceived as meanings, whose boundaries are forever expanding and whose shape is forever made anew. It is important to point out once again, however, that Benet does not propose at any point to renounce facts or to denounce science. His intention is rather to shift the focus from the imperiousness of truth to the evanescence of meaning.

The dynamism of history and historical change that Benet envisions in his theory, however, should not be confused with optimism. While Hegel (whose ideas on history are clearly present in Benet) identified recurrent historical change with the progress of humankind to higher levels of rationality and therefore to freedom, Benet views history as a persistent dilation of tragedy. Raymond Aron has referred to such thinking as the "philosophy of becoming and not of evolution" (in Schaff 161) because it rejects the cumulativeness of truths and therefore of progress. Benet embraces such a view from a dual perspective. First, as we have seen, while offering an intellectual nod to the power of reason, he evokes all that stands outside of rationality:

> No matter how obvious the progress of our spirit and well-being may be, no matter how constant and systematic the advances in scientific procedure and the increase in its authority, all of opera [i.e., history], which is composed of a series of tragedies, exudes that gloomy, sinister, and scarcely consoling character which is independent of . . . the triumph of the light of reason over the darkness of the instincts. (*Puerta* 191)

This holds for Benet not only in an ontological sense (i.e., the zone of shadows does indeed exist), but in a temporal / narrative one as well. Time lies at the very core of narration for Benet, and in the context of tragedy it is perceived as highly corrosive. Hence the pathos of being "in time" is nothing less than the despair of being in history, which, as Hayden White points out, "cannot be absorbed by human thought except in the form of an enigma" (*Content* 181). This of course brings us full circle in Benet, from the zone of shadows to rational truth and then back again. But importantly, this movement cannot be perceived as a triumphant advance to a superior end (the end of history), but rather as an affirmation of the ongoingness of an enigmatic process. For Benet, clearly, enigma cannot be resolved by rational discourse and scientific explanation. It can be explored, however (as White writes in another context), "in symbolic thought and given a real, if only provisional, comprehensibility in those true allegories of time that we call narrative histories. Their truth resides not only in their fidelity to the facts of given individual or collective lives but also, and most importantly, in their faithfulness to that vision of human life informing the poetic genre of tragedy. In this respect, the symbolic content of narrative history, the content of its form, is the tragic vision itself" (*Content* 181). The idea of "real, if only provisional, comprehensibility" is of course crucial to Benet. It underscores the tenuousness of historical understanding and sets forth permanence as a fatal illusion. The besetting weakness of Francoist historiography, as I have suggested, lies precisely in its attempt to make a collective fact from a cultural invention. The specific strength of Benet's view of history is that it constantly reorders chaos while recognizing that this reordering does not produce a higher (absolute) order. In other words, for Benet (paraphrasing Nietzsche's famous dictum), "we have history in order not to die of truth."

Benet therefore forcefully rejects in his writing the two predominant myths (truths) of Spanish historiography under Franco—"the fall and progress" (*Angel* 62)—and affirms that history cannot overcome the inherent tragedy of historicity. While Francoist historians repeatedly characterize the historical process as a movement from chaos to form and perceive the present as "an end point signaled by the dawning of a time of peace and prosperity" (*Puerta* 191), Benet emphasizes the persistent movement from chaos to form and *then back again*. This process bears a conflictive significance in Benet's scheme which is fully consistent with his tragic vision. On the one hand, it affirms the dynamic and enigmatic facet of historical understanding that vivifies the past and makes the human attempt to comprehend it a never-ending quest. On the other, the return to chaos inherent in history precludes a sense of triumph. As Hayden White has written (referring to Nietzsche), "only Tragedy requires a constant alternation of the *awareness of chaos* with the *will to form* in the interest of life" (*Metahistory* 340). Thus to speak of peace and prosperity as the end of Spanish history ("That is what all the textbooks end up saying" [*Puerta* 191]) strips history of its richness and complexity and denies it the sole truth that it can, in the end, teach us: "that the evolution of human societies has been, is, and will continue to be a succession of unending tragedies" (*Puerta* 191). In Benet's view of history, therefore, there is neither a space nor a time of redemption. Although the discourse of history represents a temporal figuration through which humanity seeks truth about its place in time, such discourse succeeds only in concealing the truth. Contrary to Francoist historiography, then, which sets forth the circularity of Spanish history and its return to paradise, Benet insists that there exists no final, epiphanic moment in history—only a persistent intentionality to grasp for ever-changing meanings that remain always in the "zone of shadows."

It is clear that Benet opposes the essential strategy of Francoist historiography and that he offers an alternative perspective in its place. It is also evident that history for Benet is not one thing and fiction another, but that both share certain temporal explorations and intentions within the frame of narrative discourse. Benet has written of the historian's general interest in truth of occurrence, which parallels Benet's own concern for searching out the facts of the matter. But just as he has affirmed the importance of the "dictate of facts," he has also written of his desire to eliminate from narrative "the demon of exactness" (*En ciernes* 48). Furthermore, he has asserted that "only ambiguity has the capacity to make history" (*Angel* 56). In theoretical terms, therefore, we might say that Benet offers a curious admixture of propositions that lead inevitably to epistemological oppositions, and these in turn can only be resolved (if they are to be resolved at all) within the domain of enigma. In both history and fiction for Benet, to explore the enigmatic means to narrate it, to place it amid time, to configure and emplot it, and thus to know it in a way that we can know the mysteries of life within the frame of all narrative discourse.

The question persists, however, what is it that is historical about Benet's novels, and what do they convey about history? On the simplest level, that of direct reference, Benet's concern is the Civil War. In his fiction, as in real life, the Republican forces stand against the Nationalists. In addition, his novels allude to Franco; to the General Command and various fronts of the war; to foreign troops, weapons and battlefield strategy; and to the final Nationalist victory. All of these elements are evoked in varying degrees of detail and with an air of authenticity about them that may well lead readers to conclude that, indeed, they have garnered important information and achieved clarifying insights into the complexities of the Civil War. Still, these are novels; they are *about* the Civil War, but they are fictions. Furthermore, the narrative of these works bears scant resemblance to the coherent structures of historiography as outlined by historians of the Regime. Benet spurns a clearly delineated beginning, middle, and end to his narrations, while human intentionality, the decisive impetus for all historical acts, often appears suffocated by the natural and supernatural tangles of the environment. The chaotic reality of Región, the intense contingencies of existence there, and the nihilism of time seem to suggest that the only legitimate reading of Benet's fiction must proceed from allegory rather than symbol, from some abstract meaning of a higher order rather than from representational soundness. Yet in the end precisely the opposite occurs. Despite the obstacles to history, we sense that we discover more about the war and penetrate more deeply into the writing of history from Benet's fiction than from his brief "history" published in 1976, *¿Qué fue la guerra civil?*

The reason for our sense of historical discovery turns primarily upon Benet's view of time in fiction and upon the configuration that gives his novels their specific composition. Benet's strategies for emplotting his work are complex and diverse, but for my purpose here, these strategies may be divided into two groups: those that narrate the events of the Civil War and those that do not. The two groups are clearly and purposefully demarcated in Benet's fiction and create a narrative tension engendered by their opposing schemes of configuration and reference. The juxtaposition of the two is crucial on a formal level, of course, because it brings all of Benet's narrative to the edge of metaphor. The literal sense of his discourse is shattered by the apparent incompatibility of its component parts, and a deeper (in this case, historical) reality emerges from the tension between meanings preserved by the literal sense and the new meanings derived from the perceived dissimilitude among the parts. The metaphorical undercurrent lends to Benet's historical strategies a fresh authenticity, as do all good metaphors, and moves his narrative closer to the realm of truth, both in the sense of probing reality with new semantic pertinences and in the larger frame of universal and abstract meanings.

The third-person narrator in Benet's fiction relates the story of the Civil War as if immediately present to its ongoingness. He emplots and tightly controls the telling of events and produces the illusion of pure reference. It is of course an illusion, but when set against the fragmented and wandering discourse of the nonhistorical narrative, or the ramblings of first- and second-person narration that evoke the past, the illusion appears to stand all the more firmly on the level of the real. The third-person narrator generally affirms the traditional premises of cause and effect when telling about the Civil War (i.e., he adheres to the structure of "one because of the other," which Aristotle distinguishes from "one after the other") and provides the sense of a regulated order. Benet's third-person narration largely conforms to the traditions of how the real ought to be talked about, and it generally limits the possibility of awkward questions asked by the reader about verisimilitude and truth.

Formalist and structuralist theories of the twentieth century have shown that all discourse is metadiscourse. Language is about itself as well as about what it mediates, hence narrative always reveals to a greater or lesser extent the strategies of its composition. Benet's historical narrative is most often aware of what it aspires to do, and draws upon traditional historical devices to show that it functions as history within a work of fiction. In a broad way, historical discourse is always guaranteed by metatextual announcements, by references to sources of information, and by assurances of the authenticity of witnesses. Benet's narrative is buttressed by these devices throughout. For example, in the third volume of *Herrumbrosas lanzas*, the narrator interpolates a report of data on men and armaments of the Republican army in Región (136–38). It is a strategy that in this instance puts the reader in direct contact with "facts" as if in a chronicle, and it moves the immediacy of the Republican position to the fore without the taint of narrative bias. Benet achieves the same sense of nonnarrative objectivity with the battle maps inserted at various stages of the novel.[5] The nearness in time to the events of history and the documented proof of the men and their battles serve to enhance the illusion of what is real at the level of reference.

Benet uses a similar strategy when he includes two other sets of data concerning the Civil War: the letters of Eugenio Mazón in volumes 1 and 3 of *Herrumbrosas lanzas,* and a series of footnotes that tell what happens to important individuals after the war or how a particular political problem is later resolved. The letters are important devices in these instances because they reveal the viewpoint of the present tense of the war. They are of course narrated documents and thus stand once removed from the events they describe. But they are significant to the strategy of the historian because they reveal the thoughts of a witness, traditionally relied upon to offer a first-hand (though biased) view of "real" happenings. The footnotes also enhance the authenticity of the narrative: they suggest scholarly investigation and add to the discourse an aura of seriousness of purpose. They lend as well the sense of an ending to events that are left incomplete in the main body of the text, and reveal the traditional historiographic desire for wholeness and closure.

The sense of closure and fullness in historical reporting is perhaps most clearly demonstrated in Benet's representation of the battle for Región between Republican and Nationalist forces. In *Volverás a Región, Saúl ante Samuel,* and *Herrumbrosas lanzas* Benet offers long narrative segments on the military strategy of both sides in a way that is indistinguishable from his description of the fighting in his history *¿Qué fue la guerra civil?* For example, the style, technique, and intention of the following passages, one describing events at the battle of El Jarama in *¿Qué fue la guerra civil?* and one depicting the battle for Región in *Volverás a Región,* reveal no significant difference on the face of it:

On the night of February 6 the army of Varela, under the high command of Orgaz, attacked along a front that extended from Vaciamadrid to San Martín de la Vega, with the objective of crossing the Jarama, consolidating a bridgehead on the left bank and cutting off the highway to Valencia. The maneuver included 40,000 men divided into five brigades commanded by Colonels Rada, Saenz de Buruaga, Barrón, Asensio and García Escamez, some thirty batteries and three regiments of tanks. The Republican sector was defended by a strong contingent of the Army of the Center, then under the command of General Pozas, and included several government brigades, supported by the XI and XII international brigades. Even with the initial hand-to-hand combat that the Morrocans used to secure the Pindoque and Rada bridge on the summit of the Maranosa, the attack was not a tactical surprise, and both armies quickly found themselves engaged along the entire line, with the full commitment of their troops. (¿Qué fue 39)

A first column, the strongest and placed under [Gamallo's] direct command, supported by 12/125 pieces and a few Schneiders, would turn in a southerly direction from La Requerida, after crossing the passes where he had retreated the year before, to descend into the valley along a road located between Región and Burgo Mediano, cut the highway that links them, advance toward the river, and continue its march toward Región, on both banks, no matter what the enemy's disposition might be. The second column, green troops and rear guard militiamen who had never been under fire till then, grouped around a nucleus of veterans of the Civil Guard, with two batteries of howitzers mounted on muleback and four units equipped with those first Spandau machine guns . . . had a certain defensive character and were—in accordance with the plan—to establish, more or less at the point of Doña Cautiva Bridge, a strong dual position that would attract the enemy's attention and keep busy all of its forces located upstream from that point. (Volverás 68)

These fragments (and numerous others like them) reinforce Benet's reliance on the objectiveness of the facts of history and underscore as well his belief that they bear a certain referential truth.[6] The single relevant difference (and one that is crucial from the perspective of truth of occurrence) is that ¿Qué fue la guerra civil? presents real-life events, while Volverás a Región presents invented ones. In the context of narration, however, both passages embody the principle of reference that helps to define Benet's view of language and writing. For many novelists of this period (Juan Goytisolo and Gonzalo Torrente Ballester are perhaps the best examples in postwar fiction), representation through writing seems unable to make absence a presence. I do not say this disparagingly, but rather to affirm the problematic capacity of language to represent anything at all other than itself—an idea with formalist and structuralist roots and one that was articulated in theory through the 1960s and 1970s. For the most part, however, Benet offers an opposing proposition and professes an explicit trust in language. While on the one hand he has affirmed his inability to name directly, with a sparseness of words (e.g., "There is no verb that defines the action of time flowing to the spell of those moments that whirl and curl . . . , in the chinks of a soul that retracts there is only a glimmer with exact and compromising certainty of the shadow of a passion that closes over its sensitive nodules . . . " [*Meditación* 151]), on the other hand he proclaims the capacity both to create and convey reality through the new contextualizing and sheer accumulation of words. As he asserts in *La inspiración y el estilo*, "What obstacles can prevail against a man who [with his style] is able to invent reality?" (180). The notion of invention is critical here, but it cannot be removed and isolated from reference. The events of "real" life are available to the reader in Benet's historiography as objects that have truth value in the referential world. Equally important, through a kind of second-order mimesis (second-order only with respect to the world, not in relation to the referential paradigm), the events of Benet's invented history (in *Volverás a Región, Saúl ante Samuel*, etc.) attain analogous standing within the world of his fictional discourse. In other words, Benet's intention is to create the correlative in fiction for the relationship he defines *in reality* between word and object. Language is thus perceived as symbolic discourse in Benet's novels that represents not the object per se, but the most accurate possible symbol of it within the human capacity to understand the world.[7] In this sense, the "historical" elements of third-person narration are underwritten with the same assumptions made by Francoist historiography concerning language and truth.[8]

As he has shown in his essays on fiction and history, however, Benet does not let the matter rest with the ingenuous complacency of reference. His concern with style and enigma, buttressed by an overriding absorption with time and narration, compel him to turn against the "demon of exactness" and examine history as an amorphous zone of contradictions. What is more, history emerges in his fiction (as he asserts in his essays) bound up fully with tragedy. Temporal fragmentation and the Bergsonian concept of duration shape both the structural and thematic foundation of Benet's writing, and are thus crucial determinants in his portrayal of history.

In the first place, Benet's view of time and history shows a clear concern for beginnings rather than endings. His characters are most often immersed in the past, hence the structural flow of his novels is toward an antecedent, a beginning, rather than toward the future or an end. The characters evoke and probe the past with the hope that all that has escaped them may be recovered in a reconstituted unity. As the narrator of *Una meditación* points out, the catalyst and agent for this process is memory: "I have never understood how the temporal disappearance of memory is attributed to forgetting, refuted by so many phenomena, because in the same way that sedimentary rock holds in its bosom all traces of beings who left their stamp when it was nothing but soft and impressionable clay, memory can shelter and store up everything that in its clay had the necessary consistency to leave an indelible trace" (31–32). The narrator suggests here that the flow of time is able to disperse nothing without the possibility that the mind will reconstruct it as a vital component of the present. This holds true for a character such as Marré Gamallo in *Volverás a Región,* who seeks to recoup the past by her movement through time and space, as well as for the "I" of *Una meditación* or the narrator of *Saúl ante Samuel,* who aim to recover (or invent) meaning by conjuring up and exploring events that were anterior to their own existence.

As he does with other elements of his narrative, however, Benet establishes a temporal frame for the self only to shatter it. On the one hand, the sense of the past is highly deterministic. It checks the present and appears to drive it toward a settled conclusion. On the other hand, time moves from present to past and then back again, impelled by free association and subjective memory. It thus becomes a correlative, over the course of the narrative, of an open structure of beginnings that are incapable of moving toward completed endings. Benet shows this by his recurrent insistence on the inability of memory to conjure up the whole of any past thought or event. In *Una meditación,* for example, the narrator asserts, "For memory there is no continuity at any moment: a strip of hidden time is devoured by the body and converted into a series of scattered fragments, by the work of the spirit. . . . In that way a fragmentary and disordered tale that leaps about in time and space is produced, accumulating facts, images, and impressions . . ." (34–35); or in *Volverás a Región:* "It's true that memory adulterates, enlarges, and exaggerates, but it's not just that; it also invents in order to give an appearance of having lived and departed to something that the present denies" (247, my translation). Despite their resolute efforts, therefore, Benet's characters who seek to recover time (history) cannot account for causes and beginnings, and encounter only failure in their efforts to build the present from compelling moments of the past. They exhibit a remorseless dependency on all that has occurred before them, and thus repeatedly overlap and fuse time periods as a way of resolving historical and personal dilemmas. While writers such as Faulkner or Proust bond time periods so that the past participates in the engendering of a present redeemed and made whole, Benet envisions such commingling as a medium of doom.

It is here where Benet's novels of memory (e.g., *Volverás a Región, Una meditación, Saúl ante Samuel*) differ most dramatically from those discussed in chapter 3 of this study. It is not possible for a remembering character in Benet, as with Martín Gaite in *El cuarto de atrás*, Juan Goytisolo in *Señas de identidad,* or Luis Goytisolo in *Recuento*—to be awakened to the order of the past in a transfiguring moment of comprehension. Even when the past is rejected in these novels, as occurs most acutely with Alvaro Mendiola in *Señas de identidad,* it is at least integrated (in the present) into a perceiving self that opts for denial. In contrast, Benet's characters never achieve a workable dialectic between past and future, and are unable to privilege a single or specific moment of meaning because the wholeness of the antecedent is irrevocably lost. For this reason, there are no epiphanies in Benet's narrative. History does not emerge during a compelling moment of insight, nor is it suddenly made complete. As Dr. Sebastián notes in *Volverás a Región* concerning the Civil War nearly thirty years earlier, "It's what is left over from those days, shouts, sighs, a few shots at the end of the summer . . . it's all the food of our postwar; we live on rumor and feed ourselves on intrigues, but our moment has passed now, passed forever" (223). Characters in Benet's novels in search of history thus eventually fall victim to the bad faith that an epistemological quest rooted in the past can lead to the ontological goal of being in the present and future. The narrator in *Saúl ante Samuel* puts it succinctly: "I'll have to repeat one more time all of the sentences from my memory, leaving until the end the hope of finding in my mind the sole differentiating element thanks to which today is not yesterday nor tomorrow today" (261).

Since remembering fails to restore the desired wholeness of the past, characters in Benet's novels frequently seek refuge in forgetting. Such is the case, for example, with the entire town of Región: "The people in Región have opted to forget their own history" (*Volverás* 5). This is a key passage in Benet's fiction, one that in many ways insinuates the complexity of the author's historical perspective. First, Benet makes it clear, the residents of Región are aware of being in time and therefore of being in history. Indeed, the corrosive power of time weighs heavily against them. But for Benet, to live historically is always to bear a grim burden—the burden of the past. This means, as Ricoeur points out (citing Nietzsche), that our existence becomes " 'a never to be completed imperfect tense' " (*Time* 3: 236). As set forth by Nietzsche, this idea illuminates Benet's historical perspective in both a grammatical and an ethical/moral sense.[9] The imperfect tense suggests the ongoingness central to Benet's historicist posture, and it underscores in Benet's writing an imperfect historical world—there can be no paradise and no end of history, as in the Francoist scheme, only a perpetual tragedy. To diminish the tragic burden of history we must be able to live "unhistorically" (unthinkable for Benet), which is possible only through the willed act of forgetting. For Nietzsche, humankind has the power to "grow out of itself, transforming and assimilating everything past and alien, to heal wounds, replace what is lost and reshape broken forms out of itself" (*Time* 3: 236). Forgetting the past allows such a possibility and enables a people to be healthy and productive. In the Spain of Franco, however, and within the historical perspective offered by the Regime, forgetting is alien to the myths of progress and paradise so closely bound up with history. Even though Benet's characters will the past out of memory, they cannot escape the tragedy of history, which presses harshly on the present and deprives Spain of the health that Nietzsche attaches to forgetting. In the same fashion that Faulkner portrays post–Civil War society in *Sartoris* as "silent, sickly desolate of motion or any sound" (7), Benet establishes the diseased body metaphor as the emblem of Spain's historical tragedy:

> If the postwar spirit was or wanted to be a convalescence, it was soon to be converted into a new illness that . . . became endemic . . . as was later shown in the result that worked on that body, sick and mutilated by the war, by the collection of numerous horrendous and paralyzing medicines that were administered to it in the peace that followed. (*Meditación* 88, my translation)

Within the context of the diseased body, both remembering and forgetting are shown to be failed enterprises. Both have sought unsuccessfully in time (as Foucault has studied in another context) an "abode," a place to secure being and restore all that has eluded them (Foucault, *The Archaeology of Knowledge* 12). Such an effort depends upon two elements, neither of which obtains in Benet's writing: (1) the perception that being progresses through time toward a higher level and the possibility (which Benet shows to be chimerical) that memory is able to appropriate and draw near key elements of the past, which inform and stabilize a steady center of meaning; (2) the belief that forgetting can elide the tragedy of time. For the reader, of course, any attempt by Benet's characters to stabilize meaning serves as a negative analogue of how the text properly should be read. The failure of the characters to reintegrate the past liberates the reader from discrete instances of time (i.e., the points in the hierarchy of incidents that a character's memory deems crucial) and the illusion that events can be reconstituted as they once were, as well as from the illusion that events can be effaced from being. The reader is thus able to experience the text as a kinetic shifting, as a portrayal of events clearly placed in time, but without a fixed center attached to an unswerving line of meaning. This of course is precisely Benet's point as he creates a countervoice to the historiography of the Regime. Narrative is opened to a multiplicity of possible readings in the same instant that it reveals the fallacy of pursuing in the text reliable epiphanies at particular moments of the temporal flow.

The multiple meanings that Benet attaches to history in his novels are most often ambiguous and shifty—they fail to converge into traditional unities and are often suspended amid indeterminacy. It is important to point out, however, that ambiguity is not the equal of chaos in Benet's fiction, and that elusiveness does not suggest an unfettered freedom that ruptures the parameters of meaning laid out by the text. This is so in part because of Benet's concern with sustaining the referential illusion when he depicts the events of the Civil War and his reliance upon language to symbolize the intentionality of the writer. But it is also the case that the openness of Benet's narration of the past is not an "open" openness, as occurs in many antinarrativist and postmodern texts that Raymond Federman has called surfiction. Benet's narrative is not, as Federman describes surfiction, "illogical, irrational, unrealistic, non sequitur, and incoherent" (13). What perhaps best describes the narrative strategy of Benet's novels is the idea of a "framed" openness: one that leaves gaps and open spaces, but always within the broader confines of meaning delineated by the third-person narrator. For example, Benet's characters, who are deeply immersed in time (history) are rarely designed as codified symbols or actants in a highly abstract sphere of action. They resist traditional molds and defer meaning at every turn of the narrative, but at the same time they embrace familiar social and historical functions and embody discernible lines of coherence. Their placement in the narrative is not accidental or undifferentiated, as in much postmodern fiction, but rather proceeds from a structured and ordered immersion in a world that often appears to resist order. This is most evident in the way they collaborate with style and form to reveal the recurrent historical concern of the author's writing: the entropy of a world without redemption. The elements of Benet's text may not cohere fully, as critics have frequently pointed out, and characters and events may leap and shift through time and space in order to avoid unequivocal shape at a given moment, but the authority of the narrative is ever present to show how narrative time lies always at the center of meaning, even when that center is constantly in flux.

In contrast to many modernist and postmodernist novels in Europe and America, the characters and events of Benet's fiction do not develop solely out of themselves. Two key elements of his narrative reveal how this difference obtains: (1) elements of plot rarely escape the authority and control of the narrator; (2) what takes place in time is not absolved of the need for cultural definition. Thus while Benet's characters are complex, they are not unbounded. Through the controlling presence of the narrator and the recurring agency of conjecture, Benet is able to define the parameters of sense-making without enacting the sterility of a fixed meaning. That is to say, the narrators of Benet's fiction assume the authority to manipulate elements such as the geographic makeup of Región, the interaction of characters, the conflicts of the Civil War, and the like, but do not rely on a mimetically adequate representation of the "real" world in order to evoke a single (and therefore correct) perspective from which "truth" is conceived and engendered. Unlike the social realists, who envision fiction as a deterministic corollary of history and character as the embodiment of a revealed and constant truth, Benet shapes texts and characters that undercut the presumption of a unified perceiving subject who is able to grasp a preeminent truth. This holds for the point of view offered in the text by a single or by multiple narrators, as well as for the perception of the reader whose task it is to endow the novel with meaning.

For example, in *Herrumbrosas lanzas I,* the narrator makes the following observation about Captain Arderíus, one of the principal figures in the Republican chain of command: "The plain flat cap, too sharply tilted over his right ear: was it yet another indication of his fellowship with the masses, strikingly different from the military, or did it imitate the way of putting on one's hat that he had learned on the Left Bank?" (17). While affirming neither the Captain's commitment to the masses nor his contrived imitation of stylish liberalism, the narrator clearly delineates the frame for understanding Arderíus. He is not one way or another, but a portion of each. The negative limits set by the description are able to assert where the motivation for his actions may be located, and this is achieved without compelling the reader to accept any single descriptive comment as the unequivocal source of meaning. Indeed, we later learn of the Captain's duplicitous nature (he serves the Nationalist forces as well as the Republic), but the narrative never defines clearly the motivation for his treachery nor the depth of his commitment. In fact, his actions and advice in directing the Republican offensive (in *Herrumbrosas lanzas III*) promote the view of him as a loyal officer and brilliant strategist. The Republican commander (Eugenio Mazón), who knows of Arderíus's mission for the Nationalists, is completely baffled by the unexpected turn of events, and so too is the reader.

What is important about Arderíus from the standpoint of narrative strategy, however, is that the manner of his presentation parallels the way in which Benet presents history as a whole. That is to say, when a third-person narrator in Benet's fiction offers more than a single explanation for some event of the Civil War, when he conjectures about one thing or another, it is not that he seeks refuge in chaos, or that he eschews the possibility of meaning. To the contrary, he is laying out the boundaries within which potential meanings lie. In this case, he establishes a premise (the Captain's loyalty to the Republic, then his apparent treason), only to complicate it with uncertainty. He withholds and twists information about Arderíus so as to force the reader to perceive the character from multiple and often opposing angles. Benet teases the reader with ambiguity and fosters a tension that resists all attempts to apply the Realist norms of consistency. At the same time, he disallows the openness of the memory novel, in which meaning depends solely upon the insoluble aporias of the remembering "I." The function and meaning of Arderíus therefore will be determined by each reader, depending upon how that individual pieces together other descriptions that are purposely left indeterminate. But while the narrative and its rendering of history are open to interpretation, they remain closed to unbounded speculation, because by his conjecture, by his telling of one side *and* the other, rather than of one side *or* the other, the narrator adumbrates the scheme within which potential meanings lie.

Benet also achieves diversity of meaning by using the technique of multiple explanations. In *Herrumbrosas lanzas I,* for example, the narrator observes the following concerning the political alignments of a small group of Republicans:

> As the political tendencies and affiliations of people began to take shape—more than stem from old animosities they were produced, in most cases, as a consequence of the necessary association with a party by anyone who wanted to participate in the conflict . . . or [they grew from] the reluctant abandonment of neutrality maintainable with great difficulty in such compromising times, or maintainable as the least harmful stance when one is faced with the growth of a group or an ideology viewed with displeasure, or [they stem from] the desire to save one's vexed and indecisive skin with an identification card, or because of a sincere conversion, a frequent change in an

atmosphere overwhelmed by so many doctrinaire discharges of one kind or another. (138)

Clearly, Benet wishes to advance more than a single reason for the political allegiances of the Republic, but he does not seek to privilege one reason over any other. The result is a stylistically fluid passage that disperses meaning in a number of directions, but one that flows always within the broader limits of the history Benet sets out to convey. In this instance, Benet underscores the inconstancy of political motivation, which is often misconstrued by those who portray it—as did historians of the Regime—solely as a product of commitment and passion.

One of the most important strategies that Benet uses to narrate history in his fiction, and to narrate about history, has to do with the nature of storytelling. Benet's commentaries on storytelling are highly intentional. They show how facts become part of plot and how the requirements of the reader shape the way that facts are laid out. The most revealing example of self-conscious storytelling, though there are many others in Benet's novels, is found in *Herrumbrosas lanzas II* and involves the gladiator combat of Eugenio Mazón in the mid-1800s. The narrator of the tale, Ventura León, is an eyewitness to the combat in which Mazón vanquishes the champion in Pamplona and wins renown as a man of great skill and courage. Ventura León later relates the events to the public of Región with a keen sense of emplotment and the effect that his narrative will produce. He is an "eyewitness" (92) of the action, and thus bears the authority of experiencing the reality that he relates. As Benet clearly demonstrates, however, his story turns less upon the innocence of unadulterated fact than upon the exigencies of the well-told tale. In other words, history as human intentionality yields to narrative configuration, which is determined not by the found structures within the event itself, but by the requirements of dramatic narration. For example, the "eyewitness" is forced to replace a metaphor ("[Eugenio] freed himself like a cat" [95]) when it displeases the listening public. More importantly, however, as the public learns the "story" ("historia"), but wishes to hear it repeated again and again, the narrator begins to embellish the facts: he includes details that he had previously deleted and soon begins to expand the paradigm of the story with background information from Mazón's life. Eventually the demands of the public compel León to invent a whole mode of being for Mazón. He refines the story each time that it is told until the story itself co-opts and supersedes the reality from which it was originally engendered. As León (i.e., the historian) realizes, "a good story arouses deeper emotions than the best spectacle" (99).

That such a story about telling stories is interpolated into the midst of Benet's historical narration intimates more than a plot of compelling interest. It is a simulacrum on a small scale of how configuration overrides what is given as fact, and points to the way in which the storyteller projects himself and the reader imaginatively into history in order to understand beyond the surface level of event. This is precisely what Hayden White has claimed for the historian, who necessarily creates "verbal fictions" (*Tropics* 82). These fictions in no way deny the truth value of the facts that are given, but rather appropriate them into the larger and open domain of interpretation. Narration pushes meaning beyond the specific form and content of the events at hand because it refers both *to* the events and *away* from the events as they are configured and reconfigured. This kind of split referencing of the narrative, which is particularly acute in metaphor but inheres in the sense-making process of all narrative discourse, is deeply pertinent to life as it is viewed within time and history. It is in fact a metaphor within Benet's writing for historical understanding.

Another aspect of the split reference and revealed depth of historical meaning in Benet stems from the social world of his novels. The history of Región in Benet's fiction is highly charged by external circumstances. Inner lives of the characters are closely aligned with the natural and social patterns of Región, as well as with the broader notion of history.[10] For the most part, these elements are perceived as unalterable. Characters do not impose their will on what surrounds them but, to the contrary, respond to what is insinuated by external elements. Benet's is not a fiction of manners, of course, and he has never sought to reflect contemporary Spanish society in his work by collating small perceptions of the familiar into a large portrait of the real and specific. Indeed, Benet offers scant insight into the rituals of social interaction: we know very little of what his characters eat and how they dress, or where the distinctions lie between class and gender. His novels are therefore specifically counterpoised to those of the social realists of the 1950s and

1960s, whose principal aim was to reveal the interplay of human action and social determinism, one coequal with the other in working out the meaning of life. Benet's characters, in contrast, are co-opted by a history and a society that they did not make and which they generally seem helpless to unmake. Greyness and exhaustion mark the historical moment at any given time and conspire to blight the most intimate of affections and the most private of lives. This is clearly laid out in the historical frame of the mid-nineteenth century that occupies most of *Herrumbrosas lanzas II*, in the portrayal of the Civil War in *Saúl ante Samuel* and the first and third volumes of *Herrumbrosas lanzas*, and in representations of postwar Spain in works such as *Volverás a Región* or *Una meditación*.

The result of these powerful external influences is a felt absence of randomness in Benet's characters that closely complements the control obtained by narrative conjecture, but without the corresponding deterministic meanings that shape the historical forces of social realism. On the one hand, of course, Benet's writing implies a closure of outcome for character. Life and history in Región are portrayed as deathly pale, and the beings who populate the area are weighted down by the hollow silence of existence and the laming of their personality. This can be seen readily in characters such as Doctor Sebastián and María Timoner in *Volverás a Región*, the narrator of *Saúl ante Samuel*, or Cayetano Corral of *Una meditación*. On the other hand, Benet always manages to override the closure of history and being, a posture that might compel us to believe, at first glance, that he offers optimism and hope. The openness that he proposes, however, does not imply human potential (progress, change, etc.) but rather, as we have seen, human tragedy. Benet's fiction illuminates how history is made and recorded, and much of his writing serves as a broadly conceived analogue of Spain over the past seventy-five years. In this sense—and despite his protestations to the contrary—Benet is one of the great Spanish social novelists of the twentieth century. But he is social in the same way that Faulkner or Joyce are social. His placing of people and events in Región is a way not of localizing meaning but of enlarging it. Benet describes the miserable, irrational, and often obscene world of history within the confines of Región, but the eternal truths of his position are striking. They speak not to the redemption of humankind, as in Faulkner, nor even to its

Fall, but to the way in which reality is at once static and elusive. Benet's world seems never to allow change or progress, even as it resists being defined once and for all.

Benet's fiction is an esthetic and an ethic of historical writing that sharply contests the historiography of the Regime. Historians who seek to lay out the truth of the past by equating it with meaning, and who then collapse both into the paradigm of myth, speak naively and diminish history. In Benet's writing, the puzzling problems of the fantastic, the recurrent oxymoronic constructions and contradictions, and the uncertainties of temporal shifts are all ways of opening time and history to scrutiny and exegesis. Benet's representation of past time constantly in flux, bereft of conclusive sense, reveals the need and desire to reach always for something further in the way that history is understood. This "something" is crucial for Benet, but it is not defined, and it is not definable. Benet never abandons metaphysics for pure existence in his writing, just as he never abandons narration for myth. His complex style reveals an impatience to refine and qualify in the very midst of the straightforward declaration, as if no simple statement can be trusted not to falsify the complexity of things. The recurrent need to modify, to appose, to test all of the ways to say something, without the belief that any can succeed alone, coincides with the notion that transparent meaning must be eschewed. Rather than consonance, novels such as Benet's seek resonance: deep meanings that reveal an internal mark of inexhaustibility. As I have shown, Benet's narrative does not create a series of concrete historical truths. Rather it sets forth a continuum of instants of apparent contradiction, made available through the guise of multiple voices but controlled by the stylistic consistency of narration. Thus meaning is constantly deferred in Benet's writing or, put another way, there is an estrangement from Meaning, but not from meanings.

Benet clearly rejects the smugness of a past made whole, both because of his epistemological ambivalences and because of his view of the essential contingency of narrative truth. As the narrator of *Herrumbrosas lanzas III* notes in perhaps the most lapidary summary of Benet's thinking, "Most assuredly, the final verdict concerning such a frequently disputed fact is not found, nor will it be found, in any one place, because for each moment history has many explanations" (123). Like a work of art, Benet's history requires explication and interpretation. By putting an end to myth rather than to history, Benet opens the past to rearrangement, re-presentation, and regeneration. Thus rather than equalize differences and disperse disparities, as did historians of the Regime, Benet demands that we ponder the vital discrepancies of history and historiography amid the vital discrepancies of his literary texts.

5

Postmodern

Dissidences

"Madelaine," I say. . . . "semiotics is in a position to claim that no
phenomenon has any ontological status outside its place in the particular
information system from which it draws its meaning, and therefore, all
language is finally groundless. . . . " "Yes," says Madelaine . . . ,
"but some information systems are more enforceable than others."
Alas she's right.
—Donald Barthelme, "Not-Knowing"

I have sought to show to this point that the opposition of fiction to
Francoist historiography proceeds from diversity rather than from a
single, monolithic structure of dissent. In broad terms, this means that
the truth of Spanish history as set forth by the Regime is shaken and
dispersed into multiple meanings and new historical congruences. The
opposition voiced within fiction does not imply simply the displacement of one perspective with another, but rather dictates a disruption of
the interpretive and narrative strategies upon which Francoist truth
had been founded. In each case, however, fiction still holds out the
belief that the "reality" of the past is knowable in some referential
form, even though this reality is always covered with the thick crust of

language and circumstance. In social realism, for example, linear narrations suggest a history based on traditional teleological assumptions of progression, though progression here is stripped of any notion of progress by the paradigms of cause and effect that produce only decay and despair within the sphere of the horrible. In the novels of memory, the remembering self moves to the fore as the locus of interpretation and meaning. What is remembered and written into discourse in these novels is shaped by ambivalence (both the process of remembering and the contingencies of narration generally hold certainty in abeyance), but the use of a locatable "I" as the center of meaning points to a reliance on hermeneutic codes that reveal a sustained faith in the human capacity to know and understand the past. In Juan Benet, as we have seen, the writing of history emerges as a dialectic without synthesis. Benet embraces facts as the raw material for truth of occurrence, but lays these alongside his perceptions of enigma and ambiguity, which are permanently sustained by contradictions within the real and by the stylistic complexities of his narrations. Language for Benet at once represents and constructs, and then turns back on itself to reveal its dualism. Despite the rejection of closure in his writing, however, Benet refuses to abandon discourse either to chaos or to destruction. He eschews the role of de-creator and remains attached both epistemologically and discursively to the belief that the past can be made to mean, and that it can be a formative component of the human sense of being in time.

Despite the different and even opposing propositions set forth in the fiction mentioned above, there persists in each case not only the possibility of history itself, but also of writing *about* history. In other words, what Richard Rorty has called the "compulsion of language" commingles with the "compulsion of experience" (169) to produce a form of knowledge if not self-evident in character at least bound to a representational discourse that makes some claim to the real. There is another form of narrative fiction, however, that makes no such claim to the real and, in fact, most often asserts its detachment from any reality external to its own composition. This fiction brings fully to the fore Rorty's "compulsion of language" and falls generally under the amorphous term "postmodern."[1] Postmodern fictions are of course hard to pin down (in both a definitional sense and an interpretive one). They are particularly difficult when it comes to history, since on the face of it they generally reject the very concept of history and the ways in which we have tried to write the past through the creation of narrative discourses founded on mimesis. Postmodernism is a term charged with meanings and ambiguities, and its use (and usefulness) is not confined to narrative fictions. But I wish to focus in this instance on the novel, to point out how the novel stands in relation to history and, more narrowly, to show how the postmodern novel in Spain can be perceived as an important voice of dissidence. It sets out to destroy narrative paradigms that historians rely upon to give sense to the past, reveals how this process of destruction perturbs the Francoist end of history, and suggests that refusal of the eschatological is the enabling impetus for the triumph of fiction.

To focus on postmodern narratives as a form of dissidence is in many ways to enter a conceptual and definitional minefield. In broad terms, however, we might fruitfully begin with negation, since there is no shortness of things that postmodernism wants to do away with: the reality of Truth, teleological assumptions, selfhood, totalizing metanarratives, presence, centeredness, linear succession, to name only a few. Perhaps most importantly for my purposes here, postmodern views of literature generally insist on the idea of autonomous texts. Language-as-discourse is conceived as having its own laws, which are always varied and variable across texts. Thus language is under no obligation to obey any perceived laws from the world of reference. The so-called reality of a text, and perhaps what we might also call its meanings, are merely linguistic constructs shaped and reshaped through the play of signifiers incapable of drawing into our presence anything but their own strategies of composition. These ideas of course allow historiography and fiction to bleed into one another, and even to collapse fully into a messy mass of discourse that has a tenuous hold on nothing at all other than itself. In this light, histories are little more than verbal constructs that are made as novels are made, but perhaps with greater naïveté. Because our knowledge of the past is reified by language, it is necessarily defined by absence. We are therefore left to ponder history as a kind of ontological nothingness. As Fredric Jameson puts it (summed up by David Bennett): "History has [now] become 'depthless;' the past as referent has been effaced, time has been textualized, leaving only representations, texts, pseudo-events, images without originals" (Bennett 262).

Within the broad scheme of postmodernism the writing of history most often becomes untenable, even impossible. It is at best a fanciful desire pursued with great and serious purpose, but a desire that can never be fulfilled once and for all. Such a position is of course not at all encouraging, for it nourishes the sense of obliteration and helplessness that postmodernism frequently asserts. Indeed, in much postmodern thinking, meaning itself has no meaning, and a pervasive sense of nihilism moves to the fore. In our desire for a telos that situates us in time (and therefore in life itself), we as readers may mourn the absence of the object and the privileged authority of truth and systematic knowledge. We may even lament the displacement of our perceiving self as a stable provider of meaning. But the postmodern esthetic expresses no remorse; in fact, it proposes that we surrender and celebrate. As Todd Gitlin writes, postmodernism wants us to "Make the most of stagnation . . . [and] give up gracefully" (36).

The question that arises in relation to history, however, is if we shall leave the matter here. Do we settle for absence and obliteration in discourse in the face of the human need to bring the past to the present in some form of narration and thereby gain for ourselves some sense of identity and perhaps even sanity? On the one hand, I am willing to admit to the ontological deficiency of both the literary and historiographic text. Between the fullness of the world in present time, and the attempt of language to give significance to that world in past time, there is surely a gap. But I wish to insist upon the usefulness of postmodern fictional texts as a crucial determinant in the way that we know the world and its history. This usefulness must be understood as something *more* than simply laying out the standard postmodern argument that the real is fundamentally nonsignificant, that everything is fabulation, that all narrative is masturbatory. In the broadest of terms, this *something more* that postmodernism can offer is rooted in language and narration and has to do with dissent. More specifically in the context of this study, it has to do with dissent from the normative discourse that controls the writing of Spanish history and from the correlative traditions of myth-making. Most importantly, however, it is a dissent that seeks to combat the institutional power inscribed within the historiography of the Franco regime, where rigid paradigms used to co-opt the past are now revealed as fraudulent and hollow.

One of the most complex postmodern novels in Spain that actively engages historiography in order to disrupt and disperse it is Gonzalo Torrente Ballester's *Fragmentos de apocalipsis* (1977). At first glance, the novel seems hardly an eddy of intellectual crosscurrents. With its capricious plotting, its characters who move from one narrative time and space to another as if by magic, and its commingling of manuscripts created by characters who have been earlier created by other characters, the novel appears largely parodic and playful. Certainly, this is part of Torrente's intention—he enjoys the game of fiction and plays it better than most. But he also understands the danger of overextending the game, of undoing the split-referentiality that shapes the dissident nature of postmodern fiction in relation to other texts and in relation to perceived truths. Hence what appears in *Fragmentos* to underscore the essentially nonadversarial function of postmodern literature in the way that it turns inward to be about itself, at the same time raises general questions about the nature of discourse as a sense-giving component of cognition and introduces specific questions about how the past is signified by narration.

As a writer in the process of writing, the narrator of *Fragmentos* spends much of his time thinking and imagining, and his own being naturally becomes part of his speculation within the literary frame of the novel: "between asseverations and rectifications, the truth will come out, if it does come out, and perhaps I will end up finding out what I am like" (128). The notion of finding out "what I am like" is crucial, and appears to parallel the need expressed by narrators of memory novels, who likewise set out on a journey to discover who they are. But there is a significant point of difference here, one that grows from the divergence between works that disperse the referent only to recover it in a new form (as in the novel of memory) and works that renounce the referent and celebrate its absence. This does not mean, in the latter instance, that the text turns inward and surrenders to itself, but rather that it is bound up with meaning (and in this case, with the identity of the narrator) in a different way.

The nature of the journey itself exemplifies the difference. In the novel of memory, the narrator moves through time and space to regain contact with the past, to interpret it from the perspective of later experience, and to recover it within a field of meanings whose boundaries are defined by a remembering self. For the most part in these novels, the limits of knowledge correspond to the limits of memory. Experience itself may elude full recuperation, but this stems less from the perceived imperfections of narration than from the aporias of time and the cognitive fragility of memory. In *Fragmentos,* however, the narrator proclaims that he aspires to ontological presence not through experience, but paradoxically, through language: he will create "[a] mass of words in which I myself will be located, also made into a word" (132). The overriding irony of the narrator's desire is clear in this instance, for rather than solidify the thickness of his being, he exacerbates its tenuousness. First, as a general principle, language for the narrator evokes time and space that is wholly fictitious. As he remarks at the beginning of his novel: "Nothing of what I write nor of what I have written has anything to do with reality. Its space is my imagination; its time, that of my pulse beats. If with certain words I attempt to configure images of men, it is to follow custom, but no one should take it seriously" (13). The contention here is not that the narrator imagines things that have nothing to do with lived reality (he is of course a writer and can invent anything he wants) but that lived reality cannot be co-opted and reified by narration and set forth as truth. The narrator's repeated insistence that he is nothing more than a "mass of words" (15, 16, 26, 42, etc.) underscores his dilemma as a maker of fictions who wants to pin matters down but who knows that it is beyond his reach to do so. When he reminds us at the beginning of the novel that he persists in his writing despite critical obstacles, he in effect asserts that, unlike the authority of logocentrism, where naming is the equal of creating some *thing,* naming for him is the equivalent only of naming: "Don't forget that you are a mass of words, you and I are both the same, if you divide yourself into two, we are you and I, but you can also, through will power, be you or I, with no limitations other than grammatical ones" (16).

The narrator's dilemma stems in part from his desire to place himself in time (history), only to find that time and space escape his ability to narrate them. But equally important, the novel precludes the creation of a single self to begin with. Kathleen Higgins has shown (in the context of Nietzsche's view of the subject) how the postmodernist constructs a self "who is somewhere else, someone who was someone else the last time, someone who will be someone else the next time" (192). A similar dispersion of the self occurs in *Fragmentos* not only in an ontological sense (the narrator cannot figure out who he really is and, at times, *where* he is) but also in a linguistic one. For example, on occasion in *Fragmentos* (e.g., 202), the narrator suggests that he may exist only as a thought of someone else. He is correct of course—he is an invented literary character. But we must also bear in mind that he is the inventor of that character as well as of other characters (e.g., Lénutchka, Don Procopio, Don Justo Samaniego) within his verbal system. Torrente clearly raises the Unamunian dilemma of autonomy and being here. But in contrast to Unamuno, who seeks through his fiction to cast doubt on all existence (fictional and nonfictional) and therefore to raise certain epistemological paradoxes, Torrente plays out the conflict of author and his creations always on the same plane—the literary text. On the face of it, then, Torrente makes no claims about life and how it is given sense through narrative fictions: "Literature . . . is neither false nor true, it is only what it is, literature" (380). The narrator denies the influencing constructs of any system external to the text ("only through literature can literary facts be justified" [275]), and therefore his novel becomes a statement on the internal freedom of literary composition. For this reason the narrator moves his characters through time, allows them to undergo transfigurations and to make visionary statements about God—all of which challenge reality external to the text. As Clarence Major affirms about his own writing, but which is equally applicable to *Fragmentos*, "In a novel, the only thing you really have is words. You begin with words and you end with words. The content exists in our minds. I don't think it has to be a reflection of anything. It is a reality that has been created inside of a book" (130).

Torrente's insistence on words and the coincident absence of "life" in his text returns us full circle to the question posed earlier. Does postmodern fiction offer up something other than negation? Do we simply have an implosion of textual energies in *Fragmentos* (and in other novels with similar traits, such as Torrente's *La rosa de los vientos* and *Yo no soy yo evidentemente* or Juan Goytisolo's *Juan sin tierra*) that ultimately rejects the possibility of writing history because we have no access to the real? Is postmodern writing in the end simply talk about talk, as Major claims? As I have been suggesting, I believe it is not, for the texts themselves—regardless of intrinsic intentions and paradigms—expose and controvert other ideologically charged texts that make claims upon the real and the truth concerning the past within the public domain.

One of the principal ideas that shaped the historiography of the Regime was the belief in a metanarrative capable of integrating the whole of history into a steadfast truth. Francoist historians envisioned the past as emanating from a single and incontrovertible center of essences, the totality of which was embodied by a discourse that collapsed difference into sameness. In turn, this sameness laid bare an original and transcendent meaning that was not created by historians (so they believed), but found by them *in reality*. Torrente opposes this view of historiography in several of his postmodern writings. First, he rejects the delimiting consonance of a single-voiced discourse as an overarching narrative principle. For example, while historians of the State assert that continuity, orthodoxy, and uniformity endow Spain with a sanctified essence—Calvo Serer writes, as we have seen in chapter 1, "One cannot vacillate in rejecting those elements that make themselves unassimilable into the national and orthodox unifying tradition" (Díaz 72–73)—Torrente shows how the past is open to multiple narrative possibilities. He writes in *La rosa de los vientos* (1985): "I think that I will have to tell the history of my ruination several times, although I trust that I will tell it differently each time; I mean by this, the same things with different words and from different points of view" (26). Or where Franco insists in one of his frequent speeches on the certitudes of history that "[e]verything great that exists in Spain has not been the result of chance: it has been the work of noblemen, saints, and heroes, the fruit of great undertakings, of select minorities, of chosen men" (*Franco* 96), Torrente reminds us in *La isla de los jacintos cortados* (1980) that the "truthfulness" of heroism is not found in the world but constructed within narration: "History is made by heroes, and heroes are, after all, nothing more than names and appearances, words and representations" (255). Torrente clearly counters here the notion of heroism that is central to the Regime's historical program. But he does so not to show that heroism is a deceit, or that it plays no role in our understanding of the past, but that it is necessarily shaped and defined by the practices of narration.

Francoist historiography generally commingles the mythic essence of heroism with the correlative of lofty deeds ("great undertakings," in

Franco's terms). The Reconquest of course serves as a prominent example, with Franco himself dubbed in his own time "el reconquistador" (see chapter 2). In contrast, Torrente argues for a conception of history as the random occurrence of nonessential events. He observes in *Nuevos cuadernos de La Romana,* for example, that "[m]ovements that truly impel history are obscure and collective, and frequently depend upon minimal and unforeseen circumstances that can distort a situation and move it in a direction no one wanted" (224). This idea runs throughout *Fragmentos* (as well as other works such as *La saga/fuga de J. B.* and *La rosa de los vientos*) and is seen most concretely in the way that the text revolves around serialized events from the past that bear no overt transcendence: the story of Esclaramunda, don Sisnando and the battle with the Vikings, Pablo and Juanucha, the anarchist and the archbishop, the prophecies of don Samaniego. Rather than call forth the past by adhering to a single story of grand events, which clearly reveal themselves as such, Torrente splinters the past and scatters it about his narrative landscape. The microevents of history are therefore constructed with no apparent conjuncture in time or space. In other words, the events of the past are not connected in reality but rather, if they are to be connected at all, within and as discourse. Such an approach emphasizes the writer as a fiction-maker or fabulator and draws to the fore one of the central ideas of *Fragmentos:* the fictional status of all historical narrative.

Torrente also attacks the metanarrative conception of history that lies at the heart of Francoist historiography. He does so largely through the creation of a counterdiscourse that is based upon a different set of assumptions concerning the nature and function of narration. We have already seen, for example, that Torrente emphasizes meaning as a function of textual construction rather than of referential illusion. This is especially pertinent, as I have suggested, to the displacement of a centered narrative consciousness by multiple dispersed ones able to offer diverse and conflicting perspectives at the same time. The resulting interpretive amorphousness annuls the very possibility of a coherent metanarrative that is capable of rendering a single view of history. Mirroring the dissolution both of the self and of traditional narrative principles, history now becomes a series of abrupt and inorganic ruptures that serve to reveal more a state of affairs than the answer to a coherent set of questions. This fracturing of the hermeneutic code (the wholeness of which sustains the memory novel and allows for limited meanings in the fiction of Juan Benet) is the enabling impetus for the aleatory in *Fragmentos* as well as the vatic intensity associated with the apocalypse of the novel's title.

The pluralistic conception of history as a chaos of fragments is evident in a number of ways in *Fragmentos*. First of all, Torrente generally avoids narrative structures of cause and effect, thus breaking the linear succession of events and the coincident interpretive comfort that generally follows for the reader. For example, the cathedral of Villasanta was constructed nearly a thousand years before the present time by the architect Mateo at the request of Bishop Marcelo. The building is important in the novel as space for play and irony (the current bishop plays cards there each evening with the anarchists), but it also serves to fracture nexuses of causation. Since the architect proves unable to conceive the cathedral as it is envisioned by the bishop, he is sent into the future to see how it now appears as a completed structure. As the bishop explains it, "If I send you into future time, when the cathedral is finished, you go, you copy it, and you return, and then you construct it" (179). Whether it is a character pulled from one text and placed in another, or fantastic journeys of escape that the narrator associates with his various identities, stable discursive patterns in *Fragmentos* that impel stories toward closure are cast adrift. Events with consequences or concrete acts of determination through which it is possible to delineate specific historical trajectories are alien to Torrente's narrative design. Although the reader can make links between apparently disjointed parts, the text turns primarily upon the confluence of unpredictable and indeterminate spirals of events, which produce a kind of historical vertigo.[2]

Another strategy of narration in *Fragmentos* that challenges the hegemonic discourse of traditional historiography stems from the recurrent sublation of binary oppositions. These oppositions of course form the core of the State's mythic discourse and serve to represent Spanish history as a series of inclusions (e.g., heroism, Christianity) and exclusions (e.g., secularism, Judaism). Torrente is well aware in his narrative of mythic oppositions. For example, as the narrator contemplates writing his novel at the beginning of *Fragmentos*, he outlines a Manichean world of "Good" and "Bad," "Order" and "Chaos" framed within a heroic struggle (78–82). What is pertinent about the narrator's view of this struggle, however, is that it emerges as a formal and linguistic construct of narration rather than as a reflection of real-life circumstance. Historiographers of the Regime perceived precisely such a dichotomy in history itself (i.e., it was the story that history had to tell) and offered a persistent negation of one side of the dialectic rather than a synthesis that included some aspects of both sides. Torrente similarly avoids synthesis, but for different reasons. Rather than accept one aspect of the opposition or the other, he decides instead to disallow the opposition from the beginning. He is able to do so because the dialectic holds together as a construct of his discourse rather than as a *thing* found in life. Since the narrator has written the opposition into being, he can, with a stroke of the pen, eliminate it.

But the opposition also fails in the novel as a conveyor of sense. The whole of the work is founded upon the aleatory tensions and randomness not only of structures but of meanings as well. History does not have just a double face (the Good and the Bad) but multiple faces, which resist both hierarchical ordering and transcendent subjectivities. Hence the narrator seeks to persuade his companion Lénutchka (who represents the perspectives of realist traditions in the novel) of the necessity of ambiguity: "Naturally, she is not in favor of ambiguous solutions, and she seems to advise me to make my point of view clear; but I insist on keeping it vague" (368). The narrator is fully aware of the diminution of writing and meaning that would result from his proposed oppositions, hence he chooses to reject them before they can be solidified within (and as) his discourse: "Having reread . . . what I have just written, I am not at all convinced by it" (82).

One of the prominent features of postmodern fiction that allows (and compels) it to extend beyond the intrinsic structures of its own composition is the recurrent intersection with other texts. Intertextuality of course engages both literary and nonliterary forms of discourse and is generally an invigorating process even when the intent is to subvert or parody one text or the other. In *Fragmentos,* intertextuality relates to meaning and to dissidence in a number of important ways, but I would like to focus on two particular aspects: (1) other texts that occur within the novel, which speak to the ontological uncertainty of fiction and to the authority over language; (2) the way in which the interpretation of other texts relates to authenticity and power in drawing forth the past into the present.

One of the most representative uses of other texts in *Fragmentos* has to do with the character known as Shopandsuck. In a somewhat bizarre story of intrigue and duplicity, Shopandsuck conspires to work for a figure known as el Supremo. Eventually, he serves as the Supremo's double, then imprisons his master and later is forced to flee for his life. In the present tense of the novel he is being hunted by Professor Moriarty at the request, presumably, of el Supremo. Shopandsuck's "story" is a fantastic one for a number of reasons (most prominent are the leaps in time, space, and logic that shape it), but it is a particularly compelling example of both playfulness and dissidence. In the first place, the episode urges the breakdown of cause and effect, both in linear sequencing and in traditional interpretive strategies. Additionally, it embraces fragmentation as a narrative precept and reaffirms the idea that a story is constructed with words rather than found in reality. But more importantly, the linking of verbal systems (texts) here moves to the fore as an intrinsic concern that bears directly upon extrinsic matters of power and ideology as they relate to history. This is most evident in the Shopandsuck episode when the narrator discovers that Shopandsuck himself has eluded capture but that he is somewhere in Villasanta. The challenge in tracking him down, however, is largely a linguistic one: "We know that he is somewhere in the city, although in a different language system than ours" (273). The dilemma becomes here the laying of one discourse alongside another not asymptotically, as has traditionally occurred with distinct texts, but rather of proceeding in a way that allows one text to violate the other. The notion of "violation" suggests both aggression and penetration, and this is precisely what Torrente has in mind: " 'And you are saying that [Shopandsuck] is located in a system of words?' 'Exactly. Or put another way: he invented a novel and has made himself a character.' 'The first thing to be done, then, is to destroy the language in which the novel is written' " (274). To penetrate Shopandsuck's verbal system and gain control of it is of course a way of co-opting its story and forcing it to fit into another story controlled by another narrator. This allows for the construction of new, synthetic stories, which in turn are vulnerable to invasion by other stories. The process is thus endless. But more importantly in this instance, Torrente correlates aggression with the destruction of language. Since the motivating premise of *Fragmentos* is that words are both the beginning and end of meaning, to destroy language means to destroy meaning. It is important to note, however, that Torrente's destruction does not represent a turn to nihilism. He does not opt for a rhetoric of silence (as occurs, for example, in Miguel Delibes's *Parábola del náufrago,* where the discourse of power steals language from workers and converts them into baaing sheep), but rather he ties the destruction of language to the way that it "means" within certain contexts of cultural and esthetic power. In other words, destruction in *Fragmentos* occurs at the level of sense as it has come to be publicly known in the sphere of authority, but it does not suggest a renunciation of sense as it may be constructed in other contexts.

Torrente denies the authoritative center of an interpreting "I" in *Fragmentos* in the same way that he denies authority to a centered consciousness to narrate a text from a single vantage point. He underscores the necessary openness of the text to diverse perspectives early in the novel: "I live in a world of words, they make and unmake everything as long as they are public. There is no reality other than what the public word embraces, and what it excludes doesn't exist" (132). Torrente's inclusion of the word "public" here may at first glance appear to undermine the entire foundation of the closed system of language upon which his narrative is based. He makes repeated claims, as we have seen, that his text is not anchored in reality—his words, he tells us, are simply words. But it is clear in the context of *Fragmentos* that "public" does not evoke a referent extrinsic to the text, some given reality. Rather it refers to discourse received by readers, who are compelled by the admixture of texts in *Fragmentos* to link words from one discourse with other words from other discourses. This commingling produces a kinetic shifting in the meanings that have come to be identified with particular discourses as these meanings relate to the world. In *Fragmentos,* one of the most pertinent such meanings that is interrogated and mocked stems from the metanarrativist premise and ideological foundation of historiographic authority. As the narrator notes, the giving of meaning enjoins confrontation, which in *Fragmentos* enables the possibility of "a real history that is opposed to the official one" (21–22).

One of the most celebrated and controversial novels of postwar Spain immersed both in historical dissidence and postmodern contingency is Camilo José Cela's *San Camilo, 1936* (1969). In contrast to *Fragmentos de apocalipsis*, however, whose historical and historiographic emphasis grows from the imagined world of the fantastic, *San Camilo* draws forth Spain and its past as explicit referent. Yet Cela's novel is no less paroxysmal than Torrente Ballester's in the way that it assaults historical discourse and the regulation of meaning. First of all, it disdains safe narrative schemes and linguistic paradigms that afford referential comfort in favor of aleatory word masses that set readers on their heels. It spits forth as well a scatological brutality that debases ideological orthodoxy and political correctness. What is more, it is fully aware of what it sets out to do. But the frenzied self-centeredness of the novel, coupled with the harshness of its apparent referential message concerning Spain and its history, tend to blur the parameters of postmodern exigencies. Does the work consume itself through linguistic play and compel an irredemptive nihilism? Is the novel politically and sexually obscene?[3] Does it nurture misogyny and celebrate perversion? Although *San Camilo* may foster all of these ideas to a greater or lesser degree, as critics have pointed out,[4] it is perhaps most richly suggestive when laid beside Francoist historiography. Within the dual context of narration of the past and postmodern negations, *San Camilo* emerges as an indictment of Spanish history and the way in which it has been constructed.

The temporal focus of *San Camilo* is the outbreak of the Spanish Civil War in July of 1936 (the novel's subtitle is *Vísperas, festividad y octava de San Camilo del año 1936 en Madrid* [*The Eve, Feast, and Octave of San Camilo of the Year 1936 in Madrid*]). On the face of it, the novel attacks Republican Spain as a debased, even wretched mass of sexual perversion and chaotic violence that inevitably (and perhaps necessarily) propelled the country headlong toward civil conflict. Cela shows scant regard for political posturing from either the Right or the Left, and he appears to locate a myopic and dissolute national character at the center of Spanish decay. While these aspects of the novel are indeed foregrounded and have legitimately shaped debate on its political and literary positioning in late Francoist Spain, the larger issue of historical meaning limned by the novel grows from the collaboration of differences.

In *San Camilo* Cela is supremely concerned with the historical, as in *La colmena,* but he has managed to reclaim history in a way that is counterpoised to that of his earlier novel. The narrator/protagonist of *San Camilo* faces himself in front of a mirror on the eve of the Civil War and speaks to a chaotic self about the chaos of Spain and its history. Cela does not claim here a specific power for the referential illusion, as he did in *La colmena.* Rather than suggest that narration sublimely (and accurately) reflects reality, Cela turns in *San Camilo* to the problem of interpretation and meaning. He first distorts the mirror in which his narrator seeks his identity, then alters its angle of refraction, changes its frame and blurs the reflection, and finally suggests that the mirror may not exist at all: "you never had your own mirror" (279). Cela clearly asserts that to know the historical is to mediate and to narrate it with the voice of a subject and with a language that must be one's own. History is therefore made private (and personal) in the novel, but becomes no less complicated. Indeed, privacy intensifies rather than resolves the problems of meaning and thereby reveals the response to Francoist historiography that Cela ultimately attempts to draw forth in the novel.

Most importantly, as with many other novelists of this period, he creates a discourse capable of resisting the institutional and dominating discourse of the Regime. Cela does not set out in *San Camilo* to dispute facts already known and agreed upon, or to offer new information gathered from privileged sources unavailable to others. Instead, the impetus for his view of the past stems from the postmodern emphasis on ways of speaking. In a crucial sense, therefore, Cela's transgression occurs *within* language and *as* language. For example, to the extent that the author opts for a dominant vocabulary of the scatological in the novel when speaking of the past he challenges the reigning truth of history. The metaphors of masturbation/intercourse/violence/perversion that are heaped one upon the other drive the predominant images of tradition from the previously constructed continuum of history. This occurs not necessarily through reference (i.e., Cela does not focus on heretofore unexplored events in "reality"), but through the rupturing of given semantic and narrative congruences that shape traditional historiography. Such is the case, for example, with the catenation of political violence, violent sex, prostitution, and death, the whole of which serves to deconstruct any hierarchical system of values within society and across history.

The use of familiar discursive patterns in uncommon ways serves a similar function. For example, the murder of Lieutenant Castillo of the Spanish Left on July 12, 1936, followed shortly after by the assassination of the Rightist leader José Calvo Sotelo on July 13 (and the coincident chaos of the streets) has long been held up as a powerful flashpoint for triggering the uprising of July 18 that began the Civil War.[5] In *San Camilo,* however, Cela disaffirms the historical significance of the events and corrupts their ennobling political importance by placing the two deaths alongside the death of the (fictitious) prostitute Magdalena. Cela first tells the story of the two deaths with a straightforward narration and authority that parallels the tenets of traditional representation. Yet once these events are affirmed, contingency quickly moves to the fore. In the case of Calvo Sotelo, Cela calls attention to the ambiguity of fact by inserting into his narration the voice of the people, whose understanding and beliefs undermine historical certitude:

> Lt. Castillo was killed by the Falangists . . . no sir, Lt. Castillo was killed by the Communists so they can put the blame on the Falangists, you are both mistaken, Lt. Castillo wasn't killed by either side, it was a crime of passion, oh no, it had something to do with faggots, listen, couldn't he have been hit by a taxi as he was crossing the street?, no, maybe he died of some disease and they don't want to say so. . . . (68)

More importantly, however, through a form of bathetic vitiation the historical importance of the death becomes a grotesque farce. As Lieutenant Castillo's casket is paraded through the streets of Madrid and Calvo Sotelo's body is prepared for burial, the story of Magdalena's death is interwoven between and within the death of the other two. The grim scenes of a decadent, filthy, and perverted Madrid associated with prostitution and eroticism are now tied to the martyred heroes of political conflict. On the eve of civil war, amid the bitter divisions of a city in turmoil, heroism is revealed as farce. As the narrator of *San Camilo* notes, "in our country everything starts out as heroism and ends in farce" (184).

But Cela does not let the matter rest with farce. To dramatize the historical undercurrent and to add historical poignancy and irony to the events, the statue of General Espartero (a nineteenth-century liberal military leader) oversees the entire gritty scene:

Lt. Castillo's body is passing through the Puerta de Alcalá. It is night, you know that it is night, it is still pitch black, a good time to steal to flee to sleep to love to die surreptitiously to die of fear with your head under the pillow . . . what good did it do Magdalena to smell of the seven worst smells in the world?, no good, none at all because now she is dead and lying on a marble table, matter that absorbs the disinfecting lye, waiting to be thrown into the common grave, the final bitter brothel of poor men and women, respectable or not but poor, in no whorehouse does the flesh of men and women respectable or not but poor blend more quickly or more thoroughly. . . . General Espartero, on horseback and in bronze, shows the way of the dead with the gesture of a man very much used to being obeyed, sometimes, not now at night, the little birds that pass by dump on him but General Espartero is unmoved, that means nothing, Magdalena would also be unmoved. . . . (91)

Cela's debasement of the murders of Calvo Sotelo and Castillo does more than convey a particular political view or exemplify a specific narrative technique. Above all it asserts the postmodern belief that historical change as it relates to the past (as opposed to future horizons of action) is primarily a change in the way of talking about things. Hence all history ultimately collapses into narration. In the example given above, narrational primacy is achieved by defamiliarizing juxtapositions that generate newness. The blend of politics and prostitution on the leveling plane of death, overseen by the ironic gaze of a military hero, is a way of deflating historical paradigms and recasting them into new congruences. This does not suggest that history is a fiction, a lie, but that the meaning it eventually gains is always vulnerable to relations of power ruled over by those who speak with authority. Within the frame of Francoist historiography, this means that the writing of history represents a crucial component of control. From the perspective of postmodernism this control became what Jean-François Lyotard has called a form of terrorism (63). It not only constructed a discursive system that blocked distribution of existing systems within society, it also silenced dissenting voices with the potential to create new systems.

San Camilo stands opposed to historiographic terrorism by rejecting the teleology of a universal history and by subverting the metanarrative that both shapes and sustains its very existence. Against the certainty of a mythic historiography, Cela shows how history is a struggle of simulations, none of which has any a priori license to absolute or totalizing truth. In other words, rather than rivet history to a series of enactments of key figures and events that make claims to eternal authenticity, Cela seeks to destroy the myths of foundation and essence that under Franco had collapsed into reductivist narrations of a single-voiced truth. Cela rejects the claim that history is grounded in a series of essences and proposes instead to show how history is groundless. This occurs not only through the bathetic vitiation of historical figures, as I have suggested above, but also through the erasure of sameness and the establishment of difference, which is the necessary precondition for constituting the historical.[6]

The portrayal of Republican Spain and the early days of the war in *San Camilo* embodies the broad propositions of Cela's intent. For example, the attack in Madrid by loyalist soldiers and Republican sympathizers against the rebellious troops of the Montaña Barracks is historically verifiable—it took place on July 19 and 20 of 1936 and ended with the massacre and imprisonment of many of the rebel soldiers (see Thomas, chaps. 17 and 18). Cela uses these circumstances, however, to disaffirm the myth of heroism and to underscore both the tragedy and farce of history. Rather than frame the incident with the noble endeavors of important men, Cela calls forth the random actions of the masses and unheroic dislocations of chance. Although the description is lengthy, it merits quoting:

> . . . some day history will say, some day history will probably say, and maybe it won't, that the storming of the Montaña Barracks was something like the battle of Bailén pushed to its ultimate consequences, to a paradoxical caricature of itself, stretched to its limits and even beyond, General Fanjul got the role of Marshal Dupont, the victorious host were not even under the command of a modest General Castaños, they weren't under anyone's command, orders were being given but they weren't being obeyed, it was the people who faced the Montaña Barracks, this idea of the people is very imprecise, very changeable, perhaps more than twenty or thirty thousand men, each with his moving little novel stuck to his heart, but

not a single historic name, it would be difficult to write the history of the storming of the Montaña Barracks with proper names, the storming of the Montaña Barracks was like hail, hailstones don't have names either, it was an anonymous manifold action like a hailstorm or Lope de Vega's *Fuenteovejuna*. (205–06)

The aim of this description is to controvert the historical as it has been known (i.e., to eliminate the paradigm of heroism) as well as to comment upon historiography. Since Cela insists here (and throughout the novel) that closure can never be achieved, all meaningful identity that has been linked to finality becomes something of a floating dispersal of historical debris. But not debris to be scorned and discarded as something once valuable and now useless. On the contrary, this debris (of the collective) can be reshaped again and again to construct history, which is now seen as a vast argumentative text through which meanings are forever dispersed and reconstituted.

In the context of Francoist myth, this means that the overarching consequence of dissident writing is to blast the images of repression from the perceived continuities of history. In the final narrative segment of the novel, through the voice of tío Jerónimo (and prefaced by César Vallejo's "Beware of your own Spain, oh Spain!" [281]), Cela makes the crucial point: "let us fight with couched pricks against the myths that oppress man, the flags the hymns the medals the numbers the insignia the institution of marriage the regional cuisine the public records office, you and I are obliged to fight against the artifices that adulterate man, that give his existence the color of death and his conscience the dryness of straw" (288). Cela's desire of course is to liberate history from the straitjacket of myth—not only through action but through the formative material of words. The historiographic enemy for Cela therefore becomes any attempt to account for the past through appropriation and homogenization, both of which shaped myth for the Franco regime and sustained its compulsion to unity.

Francoist historians also sought consistently to create myth through binary oppositions. On the face of it, this means that history was revealed through consideration of the Other—the antithesis to every thesis received primary consideration in order for the appropriate synthesis to set things straight. But as I have shown, Francoist historiography operated only on a simulated consideration of the Other, which was little more than an operational negation of difference that lead to exclusion. This creates what Thomas Docherty has called in another context "a scenario of deterrence" (174), in which myths are proved and validated through the marginalized Other and the feigned recognition of divergence. In *San Camilo* Cela forcefully rejects the Francoist plan and suggests that what is required is a process that distends beyond dialectics—not to achieve a watery synthesis or to produce a bland compromise, but rather to embrace diversity and allow it to prosper. Hence he presents the traditional dialectic of Right and Left, Republican and Nationalist, but then permits it to spin free of both alterity and synthesis. In *San Camilo* there is no aberration in the "other" side of difference, only difference itself and another displaced locus from which meaning may arise. Cela is fully aware of the dynamic nature of this process and identifies it with the voice of knowledge in the novel, tío Jerónimo: "your Uncle Jerónimo never gives advice to anybody, he asks questions and is interested in things but he gives no opinions or advice he doesn't seem Spanish in this respect, your Uncle Jerónimo does not deviate an inch from the route he has laid out for himself but he lets everyone else go wherever it suits him, all roads lead to freedom, that is a law of the philosophy of history which a people cannot escape in spite of all the efforts of reaction, of course" (47–48).

Cela's collapsing of dialecticity without synthesis is perhaps best exemplified on a formal level when he presents the dialectic in straightforward terms as a series of options for his main character.

Yes, you face the problem again and again and you still can't solve it, it probably has a solution but you don't know what it is. To call things by their name, not to call things by their name, to swear off all things human and divine, not to swear off all things human and divine, to go to bed with this woman who smells of grease and cologne, not to go to bed with this woman who smells of grease and cologne, this woman who smells of grease and cologne may be Magdalena, alias Inmaculada Múgica, and maybe not, to take a walk through the park and the vacant lots where couples do their inevitable dirty business, not to take a walk through the park or the vacant lots where couples do their enjoyable and inevitable dirty business that will eventually make them weak, to watch with satisfaction how they beat a child to death, not to watch with satisfaction how they beat a child to death, there are children that take forever to die, to give the finger to the cripple who sells tobacco (maybe he's a hero of some war), not to give the finger to the cripple who sells tobacco (maybe he's a hero of some war). . . . (4)

Cela is conscious of the false dialectic operating in Francoist historiography (false in the sense that the dialectic is created solely to marginalize the Other) and presents here a structural analogy without privileging one side of a proposition over another. The historiography of the Regime used hegemonic articulations to create unassailable identities. These in turn territorialized the past and insinuated discursive imperialism: writing set out to reenact the past in the mode of sameness and was able to do so through the leveling power of myth. In contrast, Cela reveals here the postmodern tendency to a diversity fully oriented toward heterogeneous discourses that speak, as Thomas Docherty has insightfully written, "always with the tongues of others in one's ear" (174). In this way Cela is able to deterritorialize history in *San Camilo.* His history is clearly constructed in the text rather than found in reality, and it thereby sets forth emancipatory possibilities previously suppressed by the myth of essential foundations and its collaborative discourses. Cela is of course fully aware that his own dissident narrative will eventually become exhausted and therefore will necessarily be superseded ("habit is despotic and dangerous, more despotic and dangerous than vice" [138]). He therefore shows in *San Camilo* that there can be no firm hold on history, only a series of gestures through which we grasp for meaning, hold it tightly for a moment, and have it finally slip through our hands. The aim is not to end history, as in Francoist historiography, but to sustain it by allowing the voices of difference to remain different.

For dissident postmodern writing in Francoist Spain (e.g., parts of works by Juan Goytisolo, Cela, Torrente, and even Delibes), the meaning of history bears the imprint of the institutional authority that engenders it.[7] This authority is of course evoked antagonistically, as occurs with other writers that I have been discussing, but in postmodern writers it creates a greater sense of anxiety. This anxiety stems in part from the fear that whatever discourse they use to construct an adversarial literature, it will be perceived merely as a formalist *proposition* rather than as discursive *opposition*. This view is perhaps best represented by Robert Scholes's designation of postmodern novels primarily as metafictional works that offer little more than "masturbatory reveling in self-scrutiny" (218). But for postmodern writers the anxiety also stems from the concern that the words they use to communicate within their narrations are in fact the words established and reiterated by the institutions of social order. Thus to use these words is both to surrender their own autonomy vis-à-vis the discourses of power and to speak in a voice that is not legitimately their own.

One of the most important examples of this anxiety is seen in the post–social realistic writings of Juan Goytisolo. Goytisolo is perhaps the best known of the Spanish novelists to assail overtly the Franco Regime and its view of a sacred Spanish history, and his fiction and essays often express outrage about writing in a language controlled by others.[8] His 1974 essay, "Writing in an Occupied Language," addresses the matter directly:

> Our Spanish language, that language we use every day, is constantly being mutilated by the Fascistic mind. And this mind controls the Government. This all-powerful force, by exercising a covert violence on the virtual significance of words and meanings, mutilates the possibilities of expression. (47)

The mention here of "all-powerful force" and "control" by the government sets the combat of dissidence squarely on the metaphorical battlefield of language. It is a metaphor sustained through much of Goytisolo's writing of this period:

> Our rigid, Castilianist language indeed demands, with urgency, the use of dynamite or a purgative. (*Furgón* 56)
>
> The world in which we live demands a new language, virulent and anarchic. (*Furgón* 56)
>
> In order to get by the obstructions it was necessary to fight, first of all, against the old artistic forms that were imprisoning us and preventing us from moving ahead. In order to criticize the reality of the country it was necessary to begin with a criticism of language. (*Disidencias* 165)
>
> In order to violate Hispanic legends, myths, and values I had to

violate language as well, dissolve everything into the same violent aggression. (*Disidencias* 292)

The attitude of a writer . . . must be that of . . . resistance and revolt through a process of rupture with the clichés and stereotypes of language, a constant battle against the myths and mental prisons to which the writer sometimes unconsciously falls victim. This is very similar to guerrilla fighting in an occupied country. ("Occupied Language" 47)

The above examples are well-known among commentators of Goytisolo's novels. They evoke in each case the desire to contest a language that has co-opted both meaning and truth, and they argue that dissent begins with the creation of a new or counterdiscourse. But two specific aspects of Goytisolo's proposition are particularly important in the context of postmodernism and historiography. First, Goytisolo shows that the Regime's language inscribes a perspective on the past that reifies the desired social order—this social order is of course desired by the Regime. The anxiousness for Goytisolo occurs when his voice is enclosed by the Regime's language. As a dissident postmodernist, Goytisolo seeks to communicate the experience of entrapment in language that extends from invented fictions to the most factually based work of history. The allusion in his writing to "mental prisons" and to artistic forms that "were imprisoning us" underscores how language is perceived as a source of power that works in complicity with other sources of power (political, economic, social, etc.) to compel the writer to speak in alien terms. This speaking is part of the process that decenters a single "I" as a reliable and stable originator of the hermeneutic enterprise, and in the place of stability locates a continuously shifting and multiple "I" that engenders discourses of dissent (as occurs in Goytisolo's *La reivindicación del conde don Julián* and *Juan sin tierra* or, as we have seen, in Torrente's *Fragmentos de apocalipsis* and Cela's *San Camilo, 1936*). In the examples from Goytisolo that I have given, this dissent is overrun with words of dynamism and violence ("dynamite," "purgative," "virulent," "anarchic," "violate," "aggression," "violent," "fight," "battle," "guerrilla fighting"), aimed at allowing Goytisolo to break from enclosure and from myth. The destructive energy unleashed in Goytisolo's novels begins and ends with words—not because he sees language merely as a vehicle for telling a story with metafictional techniques, but because he perceives discourse as a locus of power. The confrontational anger evident in much of his later fiction concentrates on writing—both of fiction and of history. Since he wants to destroy the historical writing of the Regime, he defeats the images of security and wholeness with a discourse of his own that leaves the once solid fabric of Franco's myths tattered and lifeless amid the chaos of his dissent.

Goytisolo's intention to de-create with language and to undermine the single-voiced discourse of the Regime suggests his deeply rooted mistrust of language to represent the world and to construct the multiple meanings that may be attached to it. His mistrust is derived both from a repudiation of mimesis and from the recognition that the language in which he writes is authored by the rejected Other. This dual concern defines the irredemptive nature of discourse for the postmodern Goytisolo and adumbrates how postmodern writers diverge from high-modernist ones in general (e.g., Joyce, Faulkner, Dos Passos) and from recent modernist writers in Spain (e.g., Luis Goytisolo, Martín Gaite, Benet).[9] A brief comparison of narrations reveals the extent of difference. In *A Portrait of the Artist as a Young Man*, Joyce (through his main character Stephen) voices a fear about language similar to the one expressed by Goytisolo in his essays and through the character Alvaro Mendiola in Goytisolo's trilogy (*Señas de identidad, La reivindicación del conde don Julian,* and *Juan sin tierra*). A sense of this fear runs through much of *Portrait*, but is perhaps best exemplified by Stephen's conversation with the dean of English studies. In the midst of their conversation on esthetics and metaphysics, Stephen reflects on his circumstances: "The language in which we are speaking is his before it is mine. . . . His language, so familiar and so foreign, will always be for me an acquired speech. I have not made or accepted its words. My voice holds them at bay. My soul frets in the shadow of his language" (189). Joyce clearly articulates here both the modern and postmodern anxiety of speaking in terms established by the social order and therefore of surrendering one's autonomy to an Other. In this case, however, Joyce, like other modernists, eventually offers a solution to the dilemma. This solution grows from the belief in a transhistorical plane of meaning, what Paul Maltby identifies among modern writers as some not totally defined "outside." Although this outside resists categorization in either spatial or esthetic terms, it is clear that it lies beyond "society's web of discourses [and is] premised on the assumption that consciousness transcends language" (41). From this belief comes one of the pivotal passages of *Portrait:* "When the soul of a man is born in this country there are nets flung at it to hold it back from flight. You talk to me of nationality, language, religion. I shall try to fly by those nets" (203). In other words, there is redemption for Stephen, for Joyce, and for the individual consciousness which can create a transcendent discourse. This transcendence ultimately holds out the possibility for Stephen to speak in his own voice and to encounter both meaning and truth, regardless of the language that surrounds him and entraps him. As he affirms to his friend Cranly at the end of *Portrait,* he seeks "[t]o discover the mode of life or of art whereby [my] spirit could express itself in unfettered freedom" (246).

A similar belief in redemption informs the novels of memory of writers such as Martín Gaite and Luis Goytisolo (see chapter 3), and thus distances their work from postmodern suppositions. In both *El cuarto de atrás* and *Recuento,* for example, narrational elements such as fragmentation, metafiction, and the subversive correlatives that attack order, meaning, and presence, point to a desire to break with the traditions of Realism that have made overt claims to authenticity in representing the past. Even the characters that embody these ideas attempt to disencumber themselves from all that they once esteemed in order to stand apart from the forces that have shaped them. In *Recuento,* for example, Raúl relates the desire for freedom specifically to the language of his circumstances and to the body of power identified with it. The writing that he undertakes when he is imprisoned for protesting against the Regime (the entrapment metaphor here is crucial, for it compels him to break from spatial confinement by means of artistic freedom) is revelatory:

And what he wrote there wasn't like what he had written before, when instead of imposing himself upon words, words imposed themselves upon him as a kind of objective material, in accordance, no doubt, with *the repressive role of language on personality, to the extent in which any relation between names and the things that they name is at once the expression and reflection of a certain external reality.* (621, emphasis mine)

The reference here to the repressive power of language as it stands amid a particular social order (i.e., Francoism) emphasizes the limiting capacity of discourse and the concurrent need of the writer to break from it.

Despite the desire for innovation, however, this desire does not beget annihilation. On the contrary, it holds out the possibility of transcendence through recovering an authentic past, which becomes progressively less amorphous as the remembering "I" moves closer to occupying a stable center of meaning. Hence these novels generally turn upon a crucial instance of awareness, both of the world and of the affirming power of art. This is especially the case for Raúl, who in many ways embodies the same principles laid out for Stephen in *Portrait*. The transfiguring moment for Stephen occurs when he comprehends the new course and order of his life:

> His soul was swooning into some new world, fantastic, dim, uncertain as under sea, traversed by cloudy shapes and beings. A world, a glimmer, or a flower? Glimmering and trembling, trembling and unfolding, a breaking light, an opening flower, it spread in endless succession to itself, breaking in full crimson and unfolding and fading to palest rose, leaf by leaf and wave of light by wave of light, flooding all the heavens with its soft flushes, every flush deeper than the other. (172)

Raúl's epiphany turns upon a similar discernment of the superior world of creative art. He is thus able to shed allegiances to the forces of his past, and writing becomes the only means of controverting the obscurity of existence. The final drama of his life, yet to be performed, will be an enactment of his consciousness on the stage of literary creation:

> There are . . . moments in the life of a man, because of their metaphorical power, that become a summary or compendium of all of his conscious and unconscious perceptions, the concentration, each within the other, of every implicit experience, moment, and duration, a time superior in its elasticity and breadth to chronological

time. And to get a hold on that moment, that duration, supposes a centrifugal movement, circles that expand in succession, that grow larger like ripples emanating from the spot where a rock was dropped in a pond, or as a metaphor within a metaphor creates a story. The golden moment, the sensation that by means of the written word, he was not only creating something autonomous, alive within itself, but in the course of this process of objectivization through writing, he was able at once to understand the world through himself and to know himself through the world. (*Recuento* 623)

In the face of his earlier stance against the use of language to re-present life and its history, Raúl now perceives writing as the only instrument able to anchor him to the real and to define his place within it. Freed of collective entanglements, Raúl must create himself or be lost. Hence the explicit reciprocity between writing and the creation of a stable "I" located at the center of meaning: "when the author projects himself into his work, he creates himself at the same time that he creates the work" (*Verdes* 237). Raúl finally discovers liberation as a corollary of art, which now serves not only as an enactment of being, but also as its source. In other words, art overcomes the limiting constraints of social order and power and creates a transcendent domain in which the artist asserts his connection to life from above.

In postmodern dissidence as embodied by Juan Goytisolo, Cela, or Torrente Ballester, however, there is a violent desperation rooted in the belief that language and fictionality is all there is and in the fear of being forced forever to speak in terms never their own. Furthermore, consciousness, rather than be solidified into a coherent whole or be lifted above language in the manner of modernist discourses, is now perceived as enclosed by words engendered and bounded by institutional order. And if this is the case, these novelists cannot yield language to the authority of the Other without a fight. For Goytisolo, Torrente Ballester, Cela, and other postmodernists, language has a discursive power that seeks to invent not only meaning but, more importantly, hopes to sustain the debate about that meaning as a necessary compulsion. If we as readers focus only on postmodernism in relation to metafiction and chaotic and fragmented narrative paradigms, if we see these novelists simply as fabulators who underscore absence, we miss their crucial adversarial potential. In Francoist Spain, this means at least in part the intention to undermine the hegemonic discourse of historians of the Regime. Goytisolo and other postmodernists are acutely aware that meaning is tightly bound up with narrative, but they are also aware of meaning as imbued with the tensions of power relations, with the norms of institutional authority, and with the value systems of those who speak within them. These foundations of power and values within discourse and as discourse seek to enclose and entrap writers and to steal from them what may be unique and powerful within their own voice.

One of the principal characters of Torrente Ballester's *Fragmentos de apocalipsis* (Lénutchka) argues that what is important in society is inevitably important in literature (300–01). It is not that postmodernism rejects this notion out of hand, but rather that it shifts the point of departure from the real to the narrated. In this way it opens up to scrutiny the sign systems by which we live, and it offers creative fictions that oppose publicly accepted histories that have made claims to be natural, inevitable, and even divine. The extraordinary tension that results between words that reveal their power to invent, as in postmodern fiction, and words that claim to be the equal of reality itself (as in Francoist historiography) enables us, if we perceive the tension, to understand how words situate us in the world. The double referencing by postmodern texts of other texts and of the powerful meanings that those texts are given in our lives, constitutes the principal reference of postmodern narrations. Double referencing therefore makes the postmodern emphasis on words more than a playful game of literary manipulation. It makes it, in fact, a political act of dissent.

6

Ambiguous Conclusions:

Writing and Apocalypse, or the

Triumph of Fiction

Why, then, shouldn't a "work of literature" suspend its telos?
—Ihab Hassan, *The Dismemberment of Orpheus*

One of the traditional goals of literary interpretation has been to find in a text the Jamesian "figure in the carpet." This means in a general way that the critic seeks out a paradigm of formal or thematic occurrences, allowing a coherent meaning to be ascribed to a text even when the text itself (as in much vanguardist experimentation) appears to resist coherence. Postmodern writing, however, not only thwarts coherent paradigmatic readings, it actively ridicules them. Thus when a character in a novel such as Donald Barthelme's *Snow White* asks, "Where is the figure in the carpet," the response is quickly preempted by another question that offers the only answer possible: "Or is it just . . . carpet?" (129). In other words, postmodern fiction acts to destroy formal and epistemological patterns (both of texts and of critical responses to them) and for this reason has come to be associated with subversion, with the end of things, and with apocalypse. Leslie Fiedler, for example, discusses how the antirational urges of our postmodern era and the insurgent energy of countercultures are largely apocalyptic (365), while Susan Sontag contends that postmodernism proclaims "a harsh despair and perverse vision of apocalypse" (203). Following a similar line of thought, Ihab Hassan views postmodern narratives as an expression of anarchy and a chaotic impulse toward "decreation" ("POSTmodernISM" 29).

The idea of apocalypse generally calls forth the image of a cosmic struggle in which the forces of good and evil are engaged in an irreversible fall toward cataclysm and Final Judgment. The effort to understand and explain such a fall, along with the implied aim of uncovering what it "means" in the religious or philosophical range of life, has traditionally been rooted in the abstract deliberations of eschatology and teleology. In a more specific way, of course, signs of the End have been wrapped thickly with the rhetoric of prophecy and with the admonitory stories of Biblical narration.[1] My concern with the apocalyptic here, however, has less to do with religious evocations of Judgment or with the end or beginning of a millenium than with the modern, secular sense of apocalypse as it relates to the perception of human experience and meaning within the flow of history.[2] Part of what I mean is defined by Hassan's suggestion that the apocalyptic involves a sense of outrage at the void of life as well as an expression of the fragmented chaos of human existence.[3] This is of course an expansive definition of apocalypse. It includes much of the fiction that has been written in the twentieth century, and it dramatizes the notion of apocalypse as unfettered destruction amid the nullity of existence. Apocalypse does suggest such meanings, but it also bears the meaning of revelation. And beyond what it reveals, it supposes transformation.[4] It is in this dual sense that apocalypse is identified with postmodern Spanish fiction and historiography in relation to the end of Francoism and its associated foundations of power, as well as to the narrations of dissidence. First, as an expression of despair, the apocalyptic implies the supersedence of a threshold in the strategies of narration which, as Douglas Robinson has shown, "implicates even the least destructive [texts] in the will to destroy" (236). Second, what is destroyed by these texts permits the crossing of boundaries between blindness (history as myth, as stasis) and insight (history as revelation), and thus sustains the apocalyptic as a vital construct of knowing the past.

As I suggested in chapter 1, Franco's purifying synthesis of the Spanish past was set forth as the end of history, a redemptive fall into paradise that established triumph, loyalty, and consonance as the matrix of "La España eterna" (or in Jamesian terms, it established these ideas as "the figure in the carpet"). The broad sweep of ideas associated with postmodern fiction stands opposed to such historiographic propositions to begin with, but this opposition deepens when perceived beside the correlative notion of apocalypse. On the one hand, apocalyptic narration offers a constant and recurrent sense of progressing toward an end. The movement is both temporal and moral in most cases; it is also perceived as unidirectional and irreversible. Yet closely scrutinized, the notion of finality is not really final, since at the end of things, as Frank Kermode has pointed out, there will arise "a disconfirmation followed by a consonance" (*Sense* 18), which in many instances represents a regress into the safe zone of myth. In postmodern fiction, however, disconfirmation is followed not by consonance, but by another disconfirmation, which in turn produces another, and so on, as the ongoingness of the process assumes its own self-nourishing and dispersive power. The "de-creative" component of postmodern novels enables the apocalyptic to spin loose from the mythic forces that seek always to resist it, or to defer it for another time, so that revelation is possible and transformation becomes inevitable. What is revealed in these novels, of course, in a reversal of Kermode's sense of consonance as a satisfactory ending, is the cataclysm of consonance as it relates to the writing of history; and what is transformed is consonance into dissonance. Most importantly, what is given life anew, as all apocalyptic writing implies, is meaning itself. As Kermode succinctly puts it, "Myths are the agent of stability, fictions the agent of change" (*Sense* 39). In other words, the imposition of apocalypse signals for history and for narration the end of myth and the triumph of fiction.

Two writers previously discussed here, both of whom have crafted well-known postmodern narrations, will serve to make the point. First, within the narrative schemes that validate the triumph of fiction, Juan Goytisolo offers perhaps the most decisive use of apocalypse. As we have seen, his entreaty for creative destructiveness, the putting of an end to the language propagated by the State, emerges correlatively with his dissent from "La España Sagrada." In his fiction (primarily in *La reivindicación del conde don Julián* and *Juan sin tierra*) Goytisolo speaks not so much against the myths of Spanish history as a separate or separable content, but rather addresses the nature of language and narration in which such myths are conveyed. Goytisolo's texts assert the end of the Regime's postapocalyptic order and its paradigm of truthmaking, and they do so with the promise to reveal and transform—not reveal some specific fact or transform a particular component of society, but rather the whole discourse of telling in that society. Goytisolo displays an outrage that challenges the Regime's defeat of time and change, as well as the way that the past is made known. And as Hassan has succinctly affirmed, "outrage requires apocalypse" (*Silence* 60).

The most intriguing aspect of Goytisolo's writing turns not upon whether he rails against Spain's sense of purity and continuity since its birth as a nation—his intention and achievement plainly coalesce in this regard. What must be considered is whether Goytisolo's perceived transgression in fact represents a form of narrative conformity offered in the guise of a polar opposite. In other words, does Goytisolo simply substitute a series of antimyths to counter the myths propagated by the State and thereby diminish the richness of history through a mythmaking discourse of his own? Or does he propose something quite different that strains permanently against stasis and offers revelation and transformation in its place?

Certainly at some point in his writing Goytisolo advances the same mythic inertia that he reproves in his antagonists. This is best exemplified in *Don Julián,* where parody and subversion contest Francoist ideology and counter the litany of myths (heroism, purity, stoicism, etc.) that it conveys.[5] Goytisolo embeds dissidence deeply into the core of *Don Julián* but, as Jo Labanyi observes, "[the novel] perpetuates the mythical vision that it sets out to subvert" (196). Labanyi suggests that "[h]istorical reality is excluded from the novel" (196) in the sense that myth is presented and then destroyed through a recurrent structuring of binary oppositions that leaves the text closed to dissent from Goytisolo's own dissent. But such a conclusion holds only if we limit our reading of myth to content rather than to Hayden White's "content of the form." Indeed, it is precisely the dynamism of the latter that defines the apocalyptic process through which myth is superseded by fiction.

Goytisolo gains the triumph of fiction in two complementary ways. First, through the imposition of a metafictional structure upon the foundation of myth; second, by inserting a subject (a narrating and remembering "I") at the source of his discourse whose dispersion both *by* language and *into* language wrests meaning from stability and casts it into the insurgent counterdiscourse of the postmodern. This is evident as early as the transitional novel, *Señas de identidad,* and carries through nearly all of his fiction to *Las virtudes del pájaro solitario* (1988), in which the ambiguous "he said" or the alternating of different subject pronouns reinforces the fragmented nature of the self. The metafictional norms of Goytisolo's novels—his telling about telling—have been frequently discussed, and need not be elaborated upon here.[6] What configures the norms of his writing in the context of apocalypse, however, is the crucial way in which they not only permit the superiority of fiction over history, but compel it.

Since metafictional texts beget meanings that in large part are textually and structurally motivated, they stand outside the referential illusion of traditional historical texts as well as the monologic discourse of Francoist myth. It is not that "history is excluded" from a novel such as *Don Julián* (or from *Señas de identidad* or *Juan sin tierra*), as Labanyi suggests, but that it appears in relation to other texts to lay bare both what it and those texts "really" are: a body of words bound up with a symbolic order of power that reconciles the demands of storytelling with the contingencies of truth and meaning as each relates to time. Importantly, the meanings attached to this order are neither natural nor permanent (as asserted by the Regime); on the contrary, they are constructed meanings and highly volatile when laid alongside other symbolic orders. Goytisolo necessarily assumes here the role of pasticheur (what Paul Maltby defines as "a trafficker in others' meanings" [5]) and thereby provokes the ek-stasis of postapocalyptic narrations. In this way, he does not so much reject history for myth, as he embraces history as fiction. His countermyths indeed function as vehicles of destruction, but Goytisolo also empowers narration to reveal the deceit of myth. He thus recasts the discourse of history into the discourse of fiction—a discourse that accounts for the teller(s) of the tale as well as for the contingencies of the act of telling. These in turn shape the oxymoronic imperative through which truths may be revealed and the world transformed, as the irruption of apocalypse (fiction) displaces the postapocalyptic inertia of history.

Torrente Ballester's *Fragmentos de apocalipsis* offers the most explicit rendering of the apocalyptic in postmodern Spanish fiction and will serve here as the second (but no less critical) example of the triumph of fiction. The title itself points to the aleatory nature of the text and suggests further that the apocalyptic "story" to be told in the novel is not a complete one. As I have shown, *Fragmentos* argues for multiple subjectivities at the point of origin of narration, embeds chaos at the level of story, and asserts the end of the Francoist postapocalyptic order and its paradigm of truth-making. This can be perceived as the overriding principle of narration that is threaded throughout the novel, but it moves fully to the fore in a final apocalyptic sequence that brings the work to an end without bringing it to closure.[7]

The final apocalyptic moment of *Fragmentos* occurs when all that the narrator has constructed during the course of his writing—all the words that he has used—begins to come apart:

> The first stroke of the bell sounded at dawn. The shock destroyed a few rhetorical ornaments, metaphors, and other such things. The second stroke came a minute later, and then the others followed in the same way: it was a deep sound that shook the air like a tornado, sharper than anything imaginable. Whole paragraphs, sentences somewhat less, and of course nouns and adverbs, could not tolerate the vibrations and broke apart: into fragments of sentences, into syllables, into monemes, phonemes, semantemes, so that my entire edifice of meanings was demolished. (395)

It is clear that Torrente reaffirms here the constructional impetus for his novel that is propped up wholly by language: in the beginning was the word, so too in the middle, and if the end is to come, the word itself must be both cause and consequence. It is also evident here that Torrente views the writer's task as a construction of some *thing,* an object made of "words." His evocation of "edifice of meanings" precludes the notion of language as a reflection of external reality and focuses attention on the component parts (words) used by the novelist to fulfill his writerly covenant. *Fragmentos* is concerned intrinsically with history to the extent that it relates the beginning and end of the town of Villasanta. It is concerned extrinsically with history in the way that it engages another verbal construction, the historiography of the Regime. Furthermore, it is highly metahistoriographic in the way it reflects upon how its discourse comes into being and what it actually means. Torrente's putting of an end to history at the end of his novel, however, is not the same end of history asserted by the Regime. In fact, it is precisely the opposite. Rather than engage mythic paradigms in order to make permanent a desired state of affairs, Torrente recoils from the certitude and teleology of myth and offers instead apocalypse in the full depth of its potential to transform. Thus as the narrator / novelist moves through his work, he first mutates, then destroys traditional narrative authority: "the word had been annihilated, in the End there was nothing" (396). The destruction here is not the end of things, but rather a requisite component of the ongoing construction of meaning, which is the only way for the narrator to reconstruct and to invent anew. In this way the end of *Fragmentos* strains to reveal and transform the "I" of the writer, as well as his narrations, into new verbal constructs, which in turn hold out the potential for new meanings whose own preeminence will be short-lived in the fragmented world of Torrente's perpetual apocalypse.

The final line of *Fragmentos*—"For my part, I began to ask myself about myself, and I found only words as answers" (398)—therefore promises hope rather than despair. It reminds us of two crucial determinants in the novel: first, despite the chaotic perturbations that constitute the core of *Fragmentos*, Torrente does not claim that we are connoisseurs of chaos—to do so would imply the presumption of a definitive truth that fosters the closure of myth. Second, Torrente does argue that chaos surrounds us, but he also shows that we are equipped to turn it to our favor through the revealing power of words. This means, as Wallace Stevens has so elegantly concluded in another context, that "[the] final belief must be in a fiction" (250). It means the end of stasis and the epiphany of narration. The narrative of *Fragmentos* therefore does not function through entelechy but through deferral. And what is deferred is the very sense of an ending because endings, as the mythic discourse of historiography shows, close off narrative from the prime matter of life, from the chaos that enables and compels narrative to transgress and transform.

The discourse of the postmodern novel in Spain embraces history not only to spin it loose and allow for transformation in the future, but to reverse, as Oscar Wilde put it elsewhere, "the decay of lying." For writers of these fictions the act of narration at once arrests lying and posits it (in Wilde's sense) as the anodyne of myth. Lying thus represents both the paradox and necessary tension of the apocalyptic vision, because it implies a restorative irony to revelation in which destruction is fully a reconstruction through the banishment of myth. In this sense, the apocalyptic structure and vision of postmodern novels are wholly revolutionary. They propose a radical discontinuity of history and hold out the possibility of revelation and transformation in a future Spain, whose past must be renarrated and whose present—the present of the Regime—must be compelled to supersede the postapocalyptic time of myth.

The writing of postmodern fiction thus stands as an act of dissidence built upon a desire for *something else*. But importantly, there exists a tension between the desire for that something else and its satisfaction. In other words, the postmodern sense of apocalypse is built upon the desire for desire rather than the desire for fulfillment. This means that the text is recurrently invested with meaning as it passes through various fields of the symbolic order (i.e., as it is laid beside other texts), and is therefore perceived as kinetic rather than static. In the end, dissidence in postmodern fiction surges forth to show that no discourse can claim to embody a totalizing system of meaning. On the contrary, postmodern narrations not only (as Lyotard writes) "refine our sensitivity to differences" (xxv), they also importune our celebration of difference.

Postscript

The Return of History

As I have sought to show, postmodern ideas represent both a formal and ideological attack on the discourse of Francoist historians during the late 1960s and 1970s. But it would be imprecise to conclude that postmodernism makes its way into Spanish fiction *because of* Francoist historiography or, once this historiography had lost its preclusive hold on the past in a democratic Spain, that postmodern tenets were abruptly cast aside. They became instead, as with many other aspects of the novel that I have been discussing, part of a reordering and transformation in Spanish fiction (and in Spanish culture as a whole) that is hard to pin down. No longer shaped and defined as a reaction against something outside itself (the constrictions of Francoist Spain), the novel becomes process and product of circumstances more richly compelling. Freedom and imagination, bound up with traditions that had been suppressed and willed from cultural circumstance (e.g., certain aspects of sex, politics, and religion, among others), now advance to the forefront of writing and are embodied by a panoply of narrative forms and intentions.[1]

Critical writing since the death of Franco has asserted disparate and even contradictory perspectives on the direction of Spanish fiction during the past fifteen years. Some writers have argued that the novel moves forcefully toward a more lyrical and metatextual extreme in order to reinvent the subjective and foreground the literary. Others have suggested that a more traditional concern with plot and reference has made the Spanish novel more socially centered, both as a way of embracing a less elitist reading public and of scrutinizing the problems of a democratic Spain. Still others have posited a synthesis derived from the perceived dialectic—the novel is neither pure discourse nor weighted down with reference, but rather has emerged as a congenial amalgam of opposing propositions.[2] It has not been my purpose in this study, however, to write literary history, and I do not propose to take up the task at this point. But it seems pertinent, in the way of final reflections, to comment briefly on the interplay of history and fiction since the end of Francoism, and to locate this interplay amid the novel's resistance to co-optation by an identifiable literary movement or coherent body of precepts.

Above all, it will be recalled, the historiographic component of fiction during the Franco years is shaped by novelistic intent (what novelists set out to do in a general sense) and by interpretive contextualizations (what novels came to mean when laid beside the dominant discourse of Francoist historians in relation to the past). The principal hermeneutic virtue of such a dual understanding of this fiction is that we are compelled to imagine the past in ways unimagined by those who sought dominion over it. The principal consequence, I believe, is that novels become immensely pertinent to life and to ways of speaking about life within the frame of human time. However, when both the intention of writing (writing against the Regime) and the context of reading (reading against Francoist historiography) are dramatically changed, the meanings that result, while no less complicated, suggest a relationship between fiction and history impelled less by discord than by a desire for narrations broadly conceived as open to Otherness.

This means, in the broadest sense, that in the post-Franco novel, history per se is perceived as naturally dynamic rather than sterile. It further means that the writing of history is now conceived as fully changeable. This does not suggest that political circumstance and social context no longer influence novelists seeking out the past or the ways in which readers understand it. (The very existence of a work such as Jesús Fernández Santos's *Extramuros* [1978], for example, which relates the story of two lesbian nuns in the late 1600s, depends upon the easing of censorship in Spain's new democracy.) But the return to history asserted by novelists, which is no longer articulated as a compulsion to write against orthodoxy, is free to seek new congruences without Truth being imposed from above. Context now commands an open field of dispersal that implies (and desires) the healthy vulnerability of discourses to corruption, commingling, and deconstruction.

It is clear that writers whose anti-Francoist discourse shaped their view of history from the very beginning (Juan Goytisolo, Luis Goytisolo, Benet, Fernández Santos, Martín Gaite, for example) have undergone the most visible change in what might be called the overt "Spanishness" of their historical writing. Juan Goytisolo, for example, has moved beyond his fixations with the Spanish past to incorporate a more universal vision into his writing—*Las virtudes del pájaro solitario* (1988) serves as a good example. Juan Benet turns to a past largely unrelated to Spain in *El caballero de Sajonia* (1991) to explore the historical determinations that shape the vision of Martin Luther (though in his unique way of writing, Benet continued to explore Región until his death in 1993). Even a writer such as Rafael Sánchez Ferlosio, whose general silence following the 1956 publication of *El Jarama* (paradigm of the social realistic novel) sets him apart from others of his generation, returns to history remote from Spain in his imaginative and fantastic *El testimonio de Yarfoz* (1986). And as Robert Spires has perceptively pointed out, Luis Goytisolo's *Teoría del conocimiento* (1981) posits a post-totalitarian discourse that urges fiction to move beyond the long shadow of Francoism: "What we are hearing is not the voice of Francoist or anti-Francoist authority, but the death-knell of both. . . . *Teoría del conocimiento* . . . can be viewed as a novel devoted to a historiographic revision of the conflict between Francoism and anti-Francoism" ("Mensaje social" 141–42).[3] This does not mean that the older generation of writers has severed the past from their works, or that what they perceived as an esthetic, ethical, and political imperative during Francoism should be cast aside as insignificant. But the compulsion to dissidence, which shaped their conceptual scheme of writing for nearly three decades, is now replaced by more potentially diverse contextualizations and changed literary circumstances.

While it is clear that the older generation of novelists such as Benet, Luis and Juan Goytisolo, Martín Gaite, Torrente Ballester, or Cela continues to exert a strong *presence* in contemporary Spanish narrative (though their *influence* is a matter more tenuously defined), younger writers reveal scant eagerness to follow the historiographic path laid out by these authors in the 1950s and 1960s. This is so for a number of reasons—from the changing economics of the publishing market and the easing of censorship laws to the influence of Latin American and European novelists and the generational desire for newness and difference. Perhaps most importantly, however, the intellectual formation and principal writings of younger authors have taken place largely in a democratic Spain, or at least during the final years of a less repressive period of Francoist rule. While the manifoldness of historical life was petrified under Francoism, young novelists such as Julio Llamazares (born in 1955), Antonio Muñoz Molina (1956), Raúl Ruiz (1947), and Juan José Millás (1946), or even slightly older writers such as Lourdes Ortiz (1943), Eduardo Mendoza (1941), José María Merino (1941), and Manuel Vásquez Montalbán (1939) have written conspicuously diverse narrations of the past that show no need to be legitimated through contraposition to other narrations of power.[4]

History in the post-Franco novel is therefore reinvigorated through the liberating admixture of fact and imagination, free now of censorship and myth, rather than through the more narrowly focused design of historiographic dissidence. In other words, novelists scrutinize the past primarily through reference to life as they believe or imagine it to have been, rather than through a historiographic discourse whose truth and value they often opposed. Several critics have in fact underscored how representation and creation inform the persistent emphasis on history in the Spanish novel. In a survey in *Insula* in 1990, when a number of writers were asked, "In your judgment, what are the dominant trends in current narrative?" nearly all of the answers emphasized the centrality of history. Angel Basanta, for example, noted that, "one notices the persistence of the historical novel in all of its varieties of re-creation, or less fact-based [novels] and more invention of the fabulous" (9). Andrés Amorós observed that "the historical novel is a constant" (9) in the past decade, while Carlos Galán Lorés affirmed that "the historical novel, whether as a straightforward reflection of an epoch or as a lesson brought forward into the present" (10) continues to shape the writing of many novelists.[5]

POSTSCRIPT: THE RETURN OF HISTORY

This shape is of course a malleable one. Freed from the contentious dialogue with a master discourse of history, Spanish narrative moves unconstrainedly through time and text, social circumstance and literary fashion. Readers may still make juxtapositions and consider authorial intention, but the urgency among novelists to write against the historical grain dissipates into the more amorphous field of historical writing—at times with the grain, at times against it, but always, now, disencumbered of the burden of a master history as forged by Francoism.

Notes

Introduction: Narrative Intimacies: Fiction and History

1. For an excellent discussion of the idea of "common sense" in the writing of history and fiction, see Louis Mink, "Narrative Form as a Cognitive Instrument," in *Historical Understanding*.

2. Although before the nineteenth century literature and history were generally considered to be branches of the same tree, Ranke's notion of "scientific" history gives rise to sharp disciplinary differences that have continued through much of the twentieth century. For a discussion of the history of these matters, see Robert Bremner, *Essays on History and Literature*.

3. The complex arguments linking historiography and fiction have been made elsewhere and are too lengthy to reproduce here. For the present study I have drawn particularly on the works of Hayden White and Paul Ricoeur, while the philosophical base of H. G. Gadamer's hermeneutics and Roland Barthes's writings on myth have served as secondary but no less pertinent points of departure. I refer the reader to these writers, as well as to LaCapra, Cowart, D'Amico, Gearhart, Morson, Weinstein, Seamon, Hutcheon, and Mink for significant insights into the commingling of history and fiction and the way in which our knowledge of the past is shaped.

4. For a highly illuminating essay on the nature of "facts" in historical writing, see Carl Becker's "What Are Historical Facts?" in which he explores three principal questions: "1) What is the historical fact? 2) Where is the historical fact? 3) When is the historical fact?" (178).

5. Derrida echoes these sentiments concerning the subject: "To deconstruct the subject does not mean to deny its existence. There are subjects, 'operations' or 'effects' of subjectivity. This is an incontrovertible fact" (Kearney 125).

6. This kind of scumbling is perhaps most cogently manifest in Simon Schama's recent book *Dead Certainties*. Schama, a historian, explores two historical events (the death of James Wolfe at the battle of Quebec in 1759 and the murder of George Parkman in Boston in 1849), not with the intention to set the "facts" straight, but to ponder the way in which the past is appropriated and given meaning. *Dead Certainties* (subtitled *Unwarranted Speculations*) is properly neither history nor fiction, but rather, as described in the *New York Times Book Review* (23 June 1991), "[a]n . . . experiment in historical narration" (4) that scumbles the disciplinary boundaries of academic tradition and calls into doubt commonsense beliefs about our knowledge of the past.

7. Little is to be gained by covering here, in a short space, the full range of studies that address history in postwar Spanish fiction. As I have been suggesting, these studies in general are of two types: (1) they use history as a backdrop against which themes and ideas of particular works are placed in order to reveal what is perceived as historical content; (2) they draw upon historical circumstances external to the text that have shaped the production of a work and are therefore implied in its meaning. It is not my purpose to dismiss these critical studies or to diminish their value, but to suggest that the present study diverges from them in significant theoretical and methodological ways.

1. Co-opting the Past: Historiography in Francoist Spain

1. For pertinent information on the history of ideas under Franco, as well as insight into the development of contemporary Spanish historiography, see Elías Díaz; Manuel Tuñón de Lara (*Metodología* and "Problemas"); Tuñón de Lara and José Antonio Biescas. Spanish historiography has of course changed dramatically in the post-Franco era. In July of 1993, for example, the Magazine section of *El País, Temas de Nuestra Epoca*, devoted the entire issue to the topic "¿La historia en crisis?" ("¿La historia?"). Several historians wrote brief essays on the problems of historiography and the incorporation of traditionally nonhistorical discourses into the study of the past. The essays themselves serve primarily to lay out crucial issues rather than to advance our understanding of theoretical matters. What is important about the magazine, however, is that it reveals the acute awareness among Spanish historians of

important disciplinary changes and of the benefits of examining the past with the aid of new historiographic principles.

2. For an excellent discussion of government control over institutions supported by the State, as well as the diffusion of the Francoist position within Spanish thought as a whole, see Díaz, chapters 2 and 3. See also Pasamar Alzuria for a discussion of how the Consejo Superior de Investigaciones Científicas influenced historiography during the 1940s and 1950s.

3. For an overview of the history of *Arbor*, see Pérez Embid, "Breve historia de la revista *Arbor*."

4. José Antonio Biescas notes concerning the role of *Arbor* that "[the magazine] represented for a long time the counterrevolutionary, national-Catholic line and set out to be a force of contention against what some considered to be the 'liberal' inconstancies (today one would say 'aperturist') of *Escorial* and *Revista de Estudios Políticos*" (Tuñón de Lara and Biescas 445).

5. For a discussion of Menéndez y Pelayo and his disagreement with the Krausists and the Institución Libre de Enseñanza, see Calvo Serer, "La significación cultural de Menéndez y Pelayo y la 'Historia de su fama,'" especially pages 311–318.

6. See, for example, the studies of José María García Escudero, Ramón Menéndez Pidal, and Fray Justo Pérez Urbel. Nearly all of the political and historical journals in Spain published special articles on Castile in 1944, and the critical role of the region in Spanish history was debated by a wide range of intellectuals.

7. It is difficult to identify the origins of the "heroic" interpretation of Spanish history among Francoist historians, but Pasamar Alzuria suggests that the concept stems from the work of Adolph Schulten, whose writings were translated into Spanish in the 1920s. More specifically, Pasamar Alzuria alludes to the Spanish translations *Tartessos* (1924), *Sertorio* (1949), and *Historia de Numancia* (1945) as highly pertinent to the notion that history is made by great men, heroes, and saints.

8. Berdyaev was read principally in French, Spanish, and Portuguese in Spain during the late 1930s and 1940s. His two most important works translated into Spanish during the decade are *La destinación del hombre* (1948) and *El sentido de la historia* (1943). In 1938 he published in Spain *Una nueva edad media* and *El cristianismo y la lucha de clases*. See *Biblioteca Hispana* throughout the 1940s for more complete bibliographic information on Berdyaev's publications in Spain.

9. Américo Castro also entered into a contentious debate with Claudio Sánchez Albornoz over Spanish history. Interestingly, the debate bears little upon the issue of writing history as propounded by the Regime, but rather has to do

with a particular meaning attached to history formulated in Castro's 1948 book *España en su historia* (second edition in 1953, with the title changed to *La realidad histórica de España* along with some changes in substance) and Sánchez Albornoz's *España, un enigma histórico* (1950). In fact, both historians are closely related to the Regime in historiographic terms. Theirs is a rhetorical history rather than a scientific one, and it conforms in many ways to the historiographic discourse set forth by the Regime. Vicens Vives sums up the matter succinctly: "It is highly unlikely that Spain is a historical enigma, as Sánchez Albornoz maintains, or a simultaneous affirmation and rejection of life ["un vivir desviviéndose"] as his antagonist affirms. Too much Unamunian anguish for a Mediterranean community with very concrete, confined, and epochal problems" (*Aproximación* 22). For additional information on the historiography of Sánchez Albornoz and his conflict with Castro, see Mariano Peset. For a broad-based attack on the ideas of Castro, Sánchez Albornoz, and the notion of an essential Spanish character, see Julio Caro Baroja.

10. Gonzalo Pasamar Alzuria sums up the single-voiced historiography of the Regime this way: "[historical interpretation] was a by-product of professional degradation, of the servile attitude of Francoist historians, and also part of the process of implementing hegemony by the victors of the Civil War. The History of Spain was reinterpreted in light of antiliberal objectives, directly or indirectly linked to attempts at intellectual elitism, to publishing and propagandistic interests in editorials, university texts, etc. As a result, with honorable exceptions, postwar historical writing connected to the professional sphere and to the world of 'national education' played the role of legitimizer of fascism" (347). Pasamar Alzuria's reference to education here is also important in the context of control over the Spanish past. For a brief discussion of the teaching of historiographic orthodoxy, see pages 302, 317, 337–38. For a more detailed view of the teaching of history during the first fifteen years of the Franco regime, see Valls Montes's *La interpretación de la historia de España y sus orígenes ideológicos en el bachillerato franquista, 1938–1953*.

11. In his discussion of Spanish history of the 1940s and 1950s, Randolph Pope points out that there was "an authentic publishing industry devoted to the Catholic Monarchs" ("Historia" 17), which cultivated a heroic and Catholic image of the origin of the nation.

12. The idea of the end of history, or of posthistory, is developed in an essay by Francis Fukuyama in 1989 to show that Western liberal democracy has triumphed over totalitarianism. I have borrowed the idea from Fukuyama to suggest that Franco viewed the triumph of his own Regime as a movement into posthistory. Of course, the Franco regime does not represent the victory of democracy, but rather the (temporary) triumph of authoritarianism.

2. Social Realism and the Myths of Historical Difference

1. The various histories of the postwar novel generally agree that social realism existed as a definable literary movement in Spain for over a decade in the 1950s and early 1960s. See, for example, Sobejano, Soldevila Durante, Corrales Egea, Gil Casado, and Sanz Villanueva, among others. I am not suggesting that all novelists writing in Spain in the 1950s adhered to the precepts or general framework of social realism, but that the writers who did adopt these precepts inscribed them rigorously in their novels during a particular period of time. For a recent attempt to reevaluate the development of social realism and its place in the history of postwar fiction, see "Revisión historiográfica del realismo social en España," the 1993 special issue of *Cuadernos Interdisciplinarios de Estudios Literarios.*

2. The writers of this group all pursued university studies in Spain during the 1940s and were directly exposed to the Regime's perspectives on Spanish history. Martín Gaite, who received her Ph.D. in history in 1972 from the University of Madrid, discusses in *Usos amorosos de la postguerra española* (1987) the importance attached to the heroic past of an imperial Spain. As she writes concerning the teaching of history in high schools, "There was not a single student in high school, no matter how little he worked, who wasn't familiar with the pictures and achievements of don Pelayo, Isabel the Catholic, or Philip II, but it was likely he had never heard of Jovellanos, Campomanes, and the Generation of 1898, unless he came from a cultured family. In any case, it didn't matter. Beginning with coverage of the eighteenth century, official textbooks had chapters just to fulfill their obligation; they scarcely contained drawings, and everyone knew they were just fluff—lessons that very rarely turned up on exams" (23).

3. On the level of theory, of course, both structuralist and poststructuralist thinking has shown the inevitable distance between signifier and signified and the destructive contingencies of a narrative founded upon the traditions of logocentrism. I do not wish to carry on the debate here concerning the ingenuousness of social realism, but rather to suggest that it lies implicit in writing at all levels, even when writers are unaware of either the cause or consequences of such thinking.

4. For an enlightening discussion of both the ethics and usefulness of intentionality in literary criticism, see Barbara Herrnstein Smith, chapter 6.

5. Fernando Morán has focused on precisely this problem when he identifies the "consciousness of historical discontinuity" (*Explicación* 60) as one of the essential components of social realism. Morán's explanation does not pursue the historiographical base of social realism, but points instead to the broad problem of alienation.

NOTES TO CHAPTER 2

6. Above all (and without devaluing the influence of traditional Spanish realism, or the importance of Italian cinema, the American Lost Generation, and a host of other factors), social realism is informed by a circumstantial imperative that motivates and defines the role of history: the opposition between the official historiography of the Regime, which eschews the notion that discourse is always a multiplicity of alternative worlds, and the dissident alternative to that historiography offered by social realism. What is of interest here is the invariable gap between the two positions and the way in which this gap informs the historicity of social realistic fiction.

7. One of the most poignant works of the 1950s to bring such a view to the fore is Sender's *Requiem por un campesino español* (1953). The novel does not fit into the social realistic mold of narration, but it underscores the hypocrisy and moral decay of the Church—a position that plainly controverts the myths of religious history propagated by the Regime.

8. Many of the ideas implicit in the narration of the social realists are in fact articulated by Vicens Vives in *Approaches to the History of Spain*. See in particular his prologue to the English translation. I am not suggesting here, however, that Vicens Vives exercised influence on the narrative strategies of the social realists.

9. For a study of how chronotope can be used to explore time/space relationships in fiction, see Clark's study of social realistic fiction in the Soviet Union. For a more theoretically oriented discussion, see Bakhtin.

10. In *El furgón de cola*, for example, Goytisolo argues, "The world in which we live demands a new language, virulent and anarchic" (93) and that "[o]ur rigid, Castilianist language demands . . . with urgency, the use of dynamite or a purgative" (94).

11. For an intelligent and complex discussion of the nature of metaphor, see Ricoeur, *The Rule of Metaphor, Time and Narrative,* and "The Metaphorical Process as Cognition, Imagination, and Feeling."

3. History and the Novel of Memory

1. I would include under the heading of novel of memory such representative works as *Volverás a Región* (1967), *Una meditación* (1970), *Cinco horas con Mario* (1967), *Señas de identidad* (1966), *Recuento* (1973), *La cólera de Aquiles* (1979), *El cuarto de atrás* (1978), *San Camilo, 1936* (1969). There are of course many other novels that could be admitted to this list, as well as related works (with complementary narrative strategies and problematic points of view) which Francisco Caudet has identified closely with the "boom" in the writing

of memoirs in the past decade—for example, J. M. Gil Robles, *La monarquía por la que luché* (1976); Carlos Barral, *Años de penitencia* (1975); Jaime Gil de Biedma, *Diario del artista seriamente enfermo* (1975); Pedro Laín Entralgo, *Descargo de conciencia* (1976); or Martín Gaite, *Usos amorosos de la postguerra* (1987).

2. The impetus for the turn from an implied consideration of history in social realism to a more overt concern in the novel of memory is hard to pin down, but there appear to be compelling reasons both literary and historical in nature. These include the failure of social realism to provoke social and political change in Spain (as it had intended), as well as the admission by many of its practitioners that social realism had scant esthetic appeal, especially when viewed in light of the innovative novels of the Latin American "boom." Within the context of literary innovation and experimentation in Spain during the 1960s, memory became a way to set loose the imagination: rather than draw out the present-day concretions of lived reality in order to understand contemporary life, novelists turned to the more malleable material of the past. But, importantly, this shift to the past allowed novelists not only to shed light on the *present*, by means of narrative and logical causality, but also to understand the *past* itself and how it gained meaning. This is especially the case in the novel of memory when the individual character moves to the fore. The increased emphasis on psychological development of the individual (as opposed to the collective protagonists of social realism) through the admixture of past and present events draws forth the question of history—both as a matter of individual knowledge and as part of the discursive practices of narration in general.

For some writers, the focus on history grew from a desire not to forget the past as the Franco regime moved to its end. For example, Jorge Semprún observed in 1989 at a symposium entitled "El arte de la memoria" that the totality of his work is an attempt to "fight against forgetting" ("Semprún" 19). At the same symposium, José F. Ivars offered a similar explanation: "The so-called 'Generation of the '50s' needs to intrude upon reality when the circumstances of our country have been de-dramatized, when the great myths of nation or honor lose part of their meaning. . . . In some way this generation feels the need to speak, from their personal situation, of human happenings that tend to disappear" (Chapa 19).

3. Much of the thinking by White, Ricoeur, and Gadamer draws upon Dilthey's writing to flesh out the fundamental issues facing both philosophers and historians as they deal with the past.

4. Goytisolo's pronouncements against the language of the Regime are well known. In numerous essays on narration and language he urges the destruc-

tion of traditional writing practices in order to subvert the power over history and culture held by the Regime. See especially the essays in *El furgón de cola* and *Disidencias*.

4. Narrative Enigmas: History and Fiction in Juan Benet

1. Both Carmen Martín Gaite and Juan Goytisolo have also demonstrated a keen interest in history and historiography. Martín Gaite received her Ph.D. in history in 1972, but in her fiction only *El cuarto de atrás* is fully engaged with history as a theme. Juan Goytisolo has been influenced by the historical writings of Américo Castro (who of course was viewed as a dissident by the Regime) and reveals this influence in his trilogy of novels, *Señas de identidad, La reivindicación del conde don Julián,* and *Juan sin tierra.* But it is Benet who engages historiography most fully in both essays and fiction and whose work turns upon the recurrent awareness of time and history as determinant factors in human existence.

2. The idea of ambiguity and enigma in Benet's writing has been examined at length in a general way, and I do not wish to cover the same ground here. My purpose is to focus on the open spaces of Benet's narrative as they relate to history. For insights into the indeterminacies of Benet's writing, both in his theory and in his fiction, see John Margenot, Malcolm Compitello, Gonzalo Navajas, Randolph Pope, and Robert Spires.

3. For a helpful overview of presentism and its relationship to positivism, see Adam Schaff, especially chapter 2.

4. The term "historicist" is both problematic and somewhat ambiguous. In the present context I use it to refer to perceptions of the past that emphasize the ever-changing and dynamic meanings of history. For an insightful discussion of historicism, see Adam Schaff (chapter 4) and Louis Mink (chapter 11).

5. For an excellent study of the role of maps in *Herrumbrosas lanzas,* see John Margenot's "Cartography in the Fiction of Juan Benet." Margenot points out how the maps at once give a referential solidity to Benet's fiction and how they undermine that solidity through contradiction.

6. In addition to *¿Qué fue la guerra civil?,* Benet treats specific aspects of the Civil War (with a similar reliance on truth of occurrence) in his essay "Tres fechas sobre la estrategia en la Guerra Civil española" (*La construcción de la torre de Babel* 85–116).

7. Benet treats the issue of the efficacy of language as mediator in several parts of *El ángel del Señor abandona a Tobías.* He is fully aware that words are not equal to objects they represent, but contends that they are at once analogous

with and generators of experience. Language is also, as Benet points out, "an instrument of communication," and "no linguist can subscribe to the conception by virtue of which language is incapable of communicating . . . " (188).

8. This does not mean, of course, that Benet attributes to facts the same meanings proposed by the Regime. Indeed, his fiction proposes precisely an opposing hermeneutic paradigm that demands alternative meanings.

9. Benet is clearly well-versed in Nietzsche's philosophy, though it would be wrong to say that he subscribes to it. Benet does cite Nietzsche at the end of *Volverás a Región* when describing the barking of dogs at daybreak: "a dog who at such hours also believes in ghosts" (285).

10. For an insightful analysis of sociohistorical influence in Benet, see Malcolm Compitello's *Ordering the Evidence*.

5. Postmodern Dissidences

1. It is not my purpose here to enter the debate over whether postmodernism "really exists," whether it is a chronological or conceptual term, or whether it can be defined with reasonable accuracy. I wish instead to show how certain esthetic and formal principles commonly associated with the term, when contextualized amid the master discourse of historiography, function to disrupt and undermine the idea of referential truth. For excellent discussions of the postmodern as a historical, esthetic, and critical concept, see Paul Maltby, Matei Calinescu and Douwe Fokkema, Ihab Hassan, J. F. Lyotard, Linda Hutcheon, Steven Connor, and Clayton Koelb.

2. In her study of myth and history in Torrente's *La saga/fuga de J. B.*, Jo Labanyi discusses how the novel offers a postmodern perspective on the circular arguments of cause and effect in the making of myth (220).

3. Paul Ilie has argued forcefully and intelligently in "The Politics of Obscenity in *San Camilo, 1936*" that *San Camilo* is both politically and ethically immoral. His assumptions are based primarily on his belief that Cela creates a mythic essence for Spain and its history that is embodied by an obscene Republic and a self-centered narrator concerned only with sexual gratification. Although Cela does indeed create both of these images, I believe that they are more fruitfully viewed (and their meanings enriched) outside the construct of myth and within the postmodern instabilities that constitute the novel.

4. In addition to the essay by Paul Ilie mentioned in note 3, see the studies by Gemma Roberts, Pierre Ullman, Jo Labanyi, and J. H. R. Polt for diverse and conflicting readings of the novel.

5. Jo Labanyi correctly points out, however, that the two assassinations did not

give impetus to the rebellion. The airplane chartered to transport Franco from the Canary Islands to Morocco had already left England to begin its journey on July 11, two days before Calvo Sotelo's murder. For a fuller explanation of these events, see Hugh Thomas, chapter 13.

6. As I mentioned earlier, Paul Ilie places *San Camilo* fully within the realm of myth. Jo Labanyi also subscribes to the mythic essence of *San Camilo,* though her reading of "meaning" in the novel is closer to my own than to Ilie's.

7. I am not suggesting here that these writers are always and at once tied to postmodern thinking. Each has passed through different phases of lengthy writing careers and has embraced different styles and theories of writing. At one time or another, however, each of these novelists has written postmodern fiction and engaged the historiography of the Regime in order to attack it.

8. I do not wish to reiterate here what others have observed concerning Goytisolo's interest in history. See the studies by Jo Labanyi and Michael Ugarte in particular for good overviews of Goytisolo's attacks on the Francoist understanding of history.

9. For insight into Juan Benet as a modernist rather than postmodernist writer, see Malcolm Compitello's essay "Benet and Spanish Postmodernism." Compitello argues that Benet pushes modernism to its limits and then reveals what these limits are, but that he never renounces the fundamental redemptive capacity of art, language, and Western rationalist thinking that would link him to postmodern ideas.

6. Ambiguous Conclusions:
Writing and Apocalypse, or the Triumph of Fiction

1. The Revelations of St. John, for example, portend chaos and order, damnation and salvation, while the Book of Daniel speaks to the cleansing of the earth and a new millennial kingdom within a temporal flow that is impelled unyieldingly toward Judgment and the Parousia. In both of these instances, and in a vast body of other exegetic texts as well, the divine and the earthly commingle within the vision of prophecy to offer the faithful an intimate and eternal knowing of God. For a good overview of these matters as they relate to literature, see Lois Zamora's *Writing the Apocalypse.*

2. From a religious perspective it would be possible, for example, to suggest in an apocalyptic context that many dissident writers in postwar Spain view Franco as the embodiment of sin and evil and that his regime is built upon cataclysm (despite, of course, what the Church might say of Franco in terms of national salvation). And from a different perspective, it would be possible

for us to scrutinize how, or how many times, narrators of the Regime draw forth the heresy or threatened victory of communism as the cataclysmic triumph of Satan. My concern here as elsewhere in this study, however, is the way in which the vision of apocalypse stands in history and in time in postwar historiography and fiction, and how it is made known through the agency of narration.

3. Hassan introduces these ideas in *The Literature of Silence* and further develops them in *The Dismemberment of Orpheus*.

4. Apocalypse comes from the Greek *apokalypsis*, which means "to uncover" or "reveal."

5. Abigail Six has commented insightfully on these matters in both her "Breaking Rules, Making History" and *Juan Goytisolo: The Case for Chaos*. Six underscores subversion and parody in Goytisolo's fiction, but does not pursue the issue through Francoist historiography. Michael Ugarte ("Juan Goytisolo: Unruly Disciple of Américo Castro") also addresses the way in which Goytisolo sets out to undermine the myths of the regime but ends up creating countermyths of his own.

6. For an insightful view of Goytisolo and metafiction, see Robert Spires's *Beyond the Metafictional Mode*, chapter 5.

7. I am using the ending of the second edition of *Fragmentos de apocalipsis*. This ending reflects the final changes that Torrente wished to make in the manuscript so that it coincided fully with the emphasis on words throughout the work.

Postscript: The Return of History

1. The easing of censorship had begun to a limited degree when the "Ley de la Prensa" was passed in 1966. With the advent of democracy following the death of Franco it was virtually eliminated. The effects of censorship are hard to measure with accuracy, but they clearly affected both writers and readers. For an overview of censorship during Francoist Spain, see Manuel Abellán's *Censura y creación literaria en España (1939–1976)*. For an overview of important themes and new narrative strategies during the first decade of post-Francoism, see Santos Alonso's *La novela en la transición*.

2. For differing positions on the development of post-Francoist fiction, see Santos Alonso's study mentioned above; Gonzalo Sobejanos's essays "Ante la novela de los años setenta," "La novela ensimismada," and "Novela y meta-novela en España"; Robert Spires's two studies "A Play of Difference: Fiction After Franco" and "Mensaje social del discurso franquista en *Juan sin tierra,*

El cuarto de atrás y *Teoría del conocimiento*"; Darío Villanueva's "Novela lírica, novela poemática"; and the special issues of *Insula* devoted to the contemporary Spanish novel, Nos. 512–513 (1989) and No. 525 (1990).

3. Spires goes on to assert in his essay that *Teoría del conocimiento* is a pivotal work for younger novelists: "And if not a direct influence, this novel by Luis Goytisolo at least helps us to understand later works whose discourse is not at all concerned with the spent conflict between the Spanish forces of fascism and communism" (142). He mentions works such as Ignacio Martínez de Pisón's *Alguien te observa en secreto* (1985), Cristina Fernández Cubas's *El año de Gracia* (1985), Esther Tusquets's *Para no volver* (1985), Antonio Muñoz Molina's *El invierno en Lisboa* (1987), and Javier Marías's *Todas las almas* (1989).

4. The following novels suggest the diversity among writers interested in the past and the possibility of a post-totalitarian discourse. I offer the list in the way of an example; it is not intended to be comprehensive: Eduardo Mendoza, *La verdad sobre el caso Savolta* (1975), *La ciudad de los prodigios* (1986); Raúl Ruiz, *Sixto VI* (1981), *La peregrina y prestigiosa historia de Arnaldo de Montferrat* (1984); Lourdes Ortiz, *Urraca* (1982); José María Merino, *El oro de los sueños* (1986), *La tierra del tiempo perdido* (1987), *Las lágrimas del sol* (1989); Julio Llamazares, *Luna de lobos* (1986); José Antonio Gabriel y Galán, *El bolo ilustrado* (1986); Antonio Muñoz Molina, *Beatus Ille* (1986); Ernesto Méndez Luengo, *Llanto por un lobo muerto* (1988); Pedro García Montalvo, *Una historia madrileña* (1988); Rosa Montero, *Temblor* (1990); Adolfo García Ortega, *Mamposo* (1990).

5. See Ignacio Soldevila-Durante's "Esfuerzo titánico de la novela histórica" for a somewhat different perspective on the continued importance of history in the Spanish novel. Soldevila-Durante puts emphasis on the fact / fiction dichotomy and the way in which the novel always is linked to what occurs in real life.

Works Cited

Abellán, Manuel L. *Censura y creación literaria en España (1939–1976)*. Barcelona: Ediciones Península, 1980.

Alonso, Santos. *La novela en la transición*. Madrid: Puerta del Sol, 1983.

Alvarez Palacios, Fernando. *Novela y cultura española de postguerra*. Madrid: Cuadernos Para el Diálogo, 1975.

Bakhtin, Mikhail. *The Dialogic Imagination*. Trans. Caryl Emerson and Michael Holquist. Austin: UP of Texas, 1981.

Barthelme, Donald. "Not-Knowing." *Voicelust*. Ed. Allen Wier and Don Hendrie, Jr. Lincoln: U of Nebraska P, 1985. 37–50.

——. *Snow White*. New York: Atheneum, 1967.

Barthes, Roland. *Mythologies*. Trans. Annette Lavers. New York: Hill and Wang, 1972.

Becker, Carl. *Essays on History and Politics*. New York: Appleton, 1935.

——. "What Are Historical Facts?" *Ideas of History*. Ed. Ronald Nash. New York: Dutton, 1969. 2:177–93.

Benet, Juan. *El ángel del Señor abandona a Tobías*. Barcelona: La Gaya Ciencia, 1976.

——. *La construcción de la torre de Babel*. Madrid: Siruela, 1990.

——. "De nuevo 'España en su historia.'" *El País* 25 Mar. 1985: 11–12.

——. *En ciernes*. Madrid: Taurus, 1976.

——. *Herrumbrosas lanzas*. 3 vols. Madrid: Alfaguara, 1983–86.

——. *La inspiración y el estilo*. Barcelona: Seix Barral, 1973.

——. "'La marcha sobre Madrid': Archivo histórico militar." *Artículos*. Vol. 1. Madrid: Ediciones Libertarias, 1983.

——. *Una meditación*. Barcelona: Seix Barral, 1970.

——. *A Meditation*. Trans. Gregory Rabassa. New York: Persea Books, 1982.

——. *Puerta de tierra*. Barcelona: Seix Barral, 1970.

———. *¿Qué fue la guerra civil?* Barcelona: La Gaya Ciencia, 1976.

———. *Return to Región.* Trans. Gregory Rabassa. New York: Columbia UP, 1985.

———. *Saúl ante Samuel.* Barcelona: La Gaya Ciencia, 1980.

———. *Volverás a Región.* Barcelona: Destino, 1967.

Bennett, David. "Postmodernism and Vision: Ways of Seeing (at) the End of History." D'haen and Bertens 259–79.

Berdyaev, Nicolas. *The End of Our Time.* London: Sheed and Ward, 1933.

———. *The Meaning of History.* London: Centenary, 1936.

Bibliografía General Española e Hispanoamericana. "A Nuestros Lectores." 13 (1941): 7–9.

Brackenridge, Hugh. *Modern Chivalry.* Ed. C. M. Newlin. New York: American Book Company, 1937.

Bremner, Robert H., ed. *Essays on History and Literature.* Columbus: Ohio State UP, 1966.

Brown, Joan. *Secrets From the Back Room: The Fiction of Carmen Martín Gaite.* University, Miss.: Romance Monographs, 1987.

Caballero Bonald, José Manuel. *Dos días de setiembre.* Barcelona: Anagrama, 1993.

Calinescu, Matei, and Douwe Fokkema, eds. *Exploring Postmodernism.* Amsterdam: John Benjamins, 1987.

Calvo Serer, Rafael. "Del 98 a nuestro tiempo: Valor de contraste de una generación." *Arbor* 12.37 (1949): 1–34.

———. "España, sin problema." *Arbor* 14.45–46 (1949): 160–73.

———. "La significación cultural de Menéndez Pelayo y la 'Historia de su fama.'" *Arbor* 20.71 (1951): 305–26.

———. "Una nueva generación española." *Arbor* 8.24 (1947): 333–48.

Caro Baroja, Julio. *El mito del carácter español. Meditaciones a contrapelo.* Madrid, 1970.

Castro, Américo. *El pensamiento de Cervantes.* Barcelona: Noguer, 1972.

———. *La realidad histórica de España.* Mexico: Porrúa, 1962.

Caudet, Francisco. "*Recuento,* de Luis Goytisolo. Análisis sociológico." *Papeles de Son Armadans* 88 (1978): 225–33.

Cela, Camilo José. "A *Mrs. Caldwell habla con su hijo.*" *Obras completas.* Barcelona: Destino, 1969. 7: 972–77.

———. *La colmena.* 9th ed. Barcelona: Noguer, 1967.

———. *San Camilo, 1936.* Barcelona: Noguer, 1981.

———. *San Camilo, 1936.* Trans. John H. R. Polt. Durham, N.C.: Duke UP, 1991.

Chapa, Ana. "Intelectuales españoles debaten sobre 'El arte de la memoria.'" *El País* 18 Sept. 1989: 19.

Clark, Katerina. "Political History and Literary Chronotope: Some Soviet Case Studies." Morson 230–46.

Commager, Henry Steele. *The Search for a Usable Past and Other Essays.* New York: Knopf, 1967.

Compitello, Malcolm. "Benet and Spanish Postmodernism." *Revista Hispánica Moderna* 44 (1991): 259–73.

WORKS CITED

——. *Ordering the Evidence: "Volverás a Región" and Civil War Fiction.* Barcelona: Puvill, 1983.

Connor, Steven. *Postmodern Culture.* Oxford, Eng.: Basil Blackwell, 1989.

Conte, Rafael. "Narrativa española de la postguerra." *Informaciones* (Suplemento de Artes y Letras) 139 (4 Mar. 1971): 1.

Corrales Egea, José. "¿Crisis de la nueva literatura?" *Insula* 223 (1965): 3, 10.

Cowart, David. *History and the Contemporary Novel.* Carbondale: Southern Illinois UP, 1989.

D'Amico, Robert. *Historicism and Knowledge.* New York: Routledge, 1989.

Davis, Lennard. *Resisting Novels: Ideology and Fiction.* New York: Methuen, 1987.

D'haen, Theo, and Hans Bertens. *History and Post-war Writing.* Amsterdam: Rodopi, 1990.

Díaz, Elías. *Pensamiento español 1939–1973.* Madrid: Cuadernos Para el Diálogo, 1974.

Dilthey, Wilhelm. *Pattern and Meaning in History.* Trans. and ed. H. P. Rickman. New York: Harper and Row, 1961.

Docherty, Thomas. *After Theory.* London: Routledge, 1990.

Eliade, Mircea. *Cosmos and History.* Trans. Willard R. Trask. New York: Harper and Row, 1959.

Esposito, Joseph L. *The Transcendence of History.* Athens: Ohio UP, 1984.

Faulkner, William. *Sartoris.* New York: Grosset & Dunlap, 1929.

Federman, Raymond. *Surfiction, Fiction Now—and Tomorrow.* Chicago: Swallow Press, 1975.

Fernández Santos, Jesús. *Los bravos.* Barcelona: Destino, 1954.

——. *En la hoguera.* Madrid: Editorial Magisterio Español, 1976.

Ferrari, Angel. Review of *Los españoles en la Historia* by Ramón Menéndez Pidal. *Arbor* 8.22 (1947): 91–113.

Ferres, Antonio. "Evolución de la novela española." *Cuadernos Para el Diálogo* 27 (1965): 25–28.

Fiedler, Leslie. "Cross the Border—Close that Gap: Postmodernism." *American Literature Since 1900.* Ed. M. Cunliffe. London: Barrie and Jenkins, 1975. 344–66.

Foucault, Michel. *The Archaeology of Knowledge.* Trans. A. M. Sheridan Smith. New York: Pantheon, 1972.

Fraga Iribarne, Manuel. "El articulado de la ley fundamental de 17 de mayo de 1958." *Arbor* 40.151–52 (1958): 515–22.

Franco, Francisco. *Franco ha dicho.* Madrid: Ediciones Voz, 1949.

——. *El pequeño libro del Pardo.* Ed. Ruedo Ibérico. Paris: Ruedo Ibérico, 1972.

Fukuyama, Francis. "The End of History." *The National Interest* 16 (1989): 3–18.

Gadamer, Hans-Georg. *Truth and Method.* Ed. Garrett Barden and John Cumming. New York: Seabury, 1975.

——. "The Problem of Historical Consciousness." *Interpretive Social Science.* Ed. Paul Rabinow and William Sullivan. Berkeley: U of California P, 1979. 103–60.

García Delgado, José Luis, ed. *El primer Franquismo. España durante la segunda guerra mundial*. Madrid: Siglo XXI Editores, 1989.

García Escudero, José María. "El concepto castellano de la unidad de España (al margen de La España del Cid)." *Revista de Estudios Políticos* 13 (1944): 150–60.

García Morente, Manuel. "Ideas para una filosofía de la Historia en España" and "Ser y vida del caballero cristiano." Rodríguez Puértolas 990–94.

Gil Casado, Pablo. *La novela social española*. 2nd ed. Barcelona: Seix Barral, 1975.

Gearhart, Suzanne. *The Open Boundary of History and Fiction*. Princeton: Princeton UP, 1984.

Gitlin, Todd. "Hip-Deep in Post-modernism." *New York Times Book Review* 6 Nov. 1988: 1, 35–36.

Goytisolo, Juan. *Disidencias*. Barcelona: Seix Barral, 1977.

——. *El furgón de cola*. Barcelona: Seix Barral, 1976.

——. *Señas de identidad*. Barcelona: Seix Barral, 1966.

——. "Writing in an Occupied Language." *New York Times Book Review* 31 Mar. 1974: 47.

Goytisolo, Luis. *La cólera de Aquiles*. Barcelona: Seix Barral, 1979.

——. *Las mismas palabras*. Madrid: Alfaguara, 1987.

——. *Recuento*. Barcelona: Seix Barral, 1975.

——. "Responde Goytisolo." *Insula* 146 (1959): 4.

——. *Los verdes de mayo hasta el mar*. Barcelona: Seix Barral, 1976.

Greenblatt, Stephen. "Towards a Poetics of Culture." *The New Historicism*. Ed. H. Aram Veeser. New York: Routledge, 1989. 1–14.

Greene, Thomas. "History and Anachronism." Morson 205–20.

Hassan, Ihab. *The Dismemberment of Orpheus*. Madison: U of Wisconsin P, 1982.

——. *The Literature of Silence*. New York: Knopf, 1967.

——. "POSTmodernISM." *New Literary History* 3 (1971): 5–30.

Herce Vales, Fernando, and Manuel Sanz Nogués. *Franco, el Reconquistador*. Madrid: Ediciones Sanz Nogués, 1939.

Herzberger, David K. "Social Realism and the Contingencies of History in the Contemporary Spanish Novel." *Hispanic Review* 59 (1991): 153–73.

——. "Narrating the Past: History and the Novel of Memory in Postwar Spain." *PMLA* 106 (1991): 34–45.

——. "History, Apocalypse, and the Triumph of Fiction in the Postwar Spanish Novel." *Revista Hispánica Moderna* 44 (1991): 247–58.

Higgins, Kathleen. "Nietzsche and Postmodern Subjectivity." Koelb 189–215.

"¿La historia en crisis?" Special issue of *Temas de Nuestra Epoca (El País)* 29 July 1993: 209.

Hutcheon, Linda. "'The Pastime of Past Time': Fiction, History, and Historiographic Metafiction." *Postmodern Genres*. Ed. Marjorie Perloff. Norman: U of Oklahoma P, 1989. 54–74.

——. *The Politics of Postmodernism*. London: Routledge, 1989.

Ilie, Paul. "The Politics of Obscenity in *San Camilo, 1936*." *Anales de la Novela de Posquerra* 1 (1976): 25–63.

WORKS CITED

Insula. Special issue on the Spanish novel. Nos. 512–513 (Aug.–Sept. 1989).

Insula. Special issue on the Spanish novel (1989–1990). No. 525 (Sept. 1990).

James, Henry. "George Eliot's *Middlemarch.*" *Theory of Literature*. Ed. J. A. Miller. Lincoln: U of Nebraska P, 1972. 152–54.

Jordan, Barry. *Writing and Politics in Franco's Spain*. London: Routledge, 1990.

Joyce, James. *A Portrait of the Artist as a Young Man*. New York: Penguin, 1983.

Kearney, Richard, ed. *Dialogues with Contemporary Thinkers*. Manchester, Eng.: Manchester UP, 1984.

Kermode, Frank. *The Genesis of Secrecy*. Cambridge: Harvard UP, 1979.

——. *The Sense of an Ending*. London: Oxford UP, 1966.

Koelb, Clayton, ed. *Nietzsche as Postmodernist*. Albany: SUNY Press, 1990.

Labanyi, Jo. *Myth and History in the Contemporary Spanish Novel*. Cambridge: Cambridge UP, 1989.

LaCapra, Dominick. *History, Politics, and the Novel*. Ithaca: Cornell UP, 1989.

Les Lettres Français, special issue on Spanish novelists, July 1962.

Levin, Harry. *Grounds for Comparison*. Cambridge: Harvard UP, 1972.

Lévi-Strauss, Claude. *The Savage Mind*. Trans. G. Weidenfield. Chicago: U of Chicago P, 1966.

Lowenthal, David. *The Past Is a Foreign Country*. Cambridge: Cambridge UP, 1985.

Lyotard, Jean-François. *The Postmodern Condition: A Report on Knowledge*. Trans. Geoff Bennington and Brian Massumi. Minneapolis: U of Minnesota P, 1984.

Major, Clarence. "Interview with John O'Brien." *Interviews with Black Writers*. New York: Liveright, 1973. 200.

Maltby, Paul. *Dissident Postmodernists*. Philadelphia: U of Pennsylvania P, 1991.

Mangini, Shirley. *Rojos y rebeldes*. Barcelona: Anthropos, 1987.

Manteiga, Robert, David Herzberger, and Malcolm Compitello, ed. *Critical Approaches to the Writings of Juan Benet*. Hanover, N.H.: UP of New England, 1984.

Margenot, John. *Zonas y sombras: Aproximaciones a Región de Juan Benet*. Madrid: Pliegos, 1991.

——. "Cartography in the Fiction of Juan Benet." *Letras Peninsulares* 1.1 (1988): 70–86.

Martín Gaite, Carmen. *The Back Room*. Trans. Helen Lane. New York: Columbia UP, 1983.

——. *El cuarto de atrás*. Barcelona: Destino, 1978.

Menéndez Pidal, Ramón. "De la vida del Cid. Notas sueltas." *Revista de Occidente* 11.32 (1934): 145–67.

——. *La españa del Cid*. Buenos Aires: Espasa-Calpe Argentina, 1939.

Menéndez y Pelayo, Marcelino. *Historia de los heterodoxos españoles. Obras completas*. Vols. 35–42. Madrid: CSIC, 1947–48.

Mink, Louis O. *Historical Understanding*. Ed. Brian Fay, Eugene Colob, and Richard Vann. Ithaca: Cornell UP, 1987.

Morán, Fernando. *Explicación de una limitación*. Madrid: Taurus, 1971.

——. *Novela y semidesarrollo*. Madrid: Taurus, 1971.

Morse, Jonathan. *Word by Word. The Language of Memory*. Ithaca: Cornell UP, 1990.

Morson, Gary Saul, ed. *Literature and History*. Stanford: Stanford UP, 1986.

Munz, Peter. *The Shapes of Time*. Middletown, Conn.: Wesleyan UP, 1977.

Navajas, Gonzalo. "The Deferred Enigma in Juan Benet's *Un viaje de invierno*." *Anales de la Literatura Española Contemporánea* 10 (1985): 41–59.

——. *Teoría y práctica de la novela española posmoderna*. Barcelona: Edicions del Mall, 1987.

Palacio Atard, Vicente. "Actitud de revancha y actitud de superación en el pensamiento tradicional." *Arbor* 14.47 (1949): 254–59.

——. *Derrota, agotamiento, y decadencia en la España del siglo XVII*. Madrid: Rialp, 1949.

——. "Menéndez y Pelayo, historiador actual." *Arbor* 34.127–28 (1956): 427–45.

——. "Razón de España en el mundo moderno." *Arbor* 15.50 (1950): 161–78.

Pasamar Alzuria, Gonzalo. *Historiografía e ideología en la postguerra española: La ruptura de la tradición liberal*. Zaragoza, Sp.: Universidad de Zaragoza, 1991.

Payne, Stanley G. "Jaime Vicens Vives and the Writing of Spanish History." *Journal of Modern History* 34.1 (1962): 119–34.

Pérez Embid, Florentino. "Ante la nueva actualidad del 'Problema de España.'" *Arbor* 14.45–46 (1949): 149–59.

——. "Breve historia de la revista *Arbor*." *Arbor* 21.75 (1952): 305–16.

——. Review of *El concepto contemporáneo de España*, ed. Angel del Río and M. J. Benardete. *Arbor* 7.21 (1946): 487–93.

Pérez Urbel, Fray Justo. *Historia del Condado de Castilla*. Madrid: CSIC, 1945.

Peset, Mariano. "Tres historiadores en el exilio: Rafael Altamira, José Maria Ots Capdequí y Claudio Sánchez-Albornoz." García Delgado 211–43.

Polt, J. R. H. "Cela's *San Camilo, 1936* as Anti-History." *Anales de Literatura Española* 6 (1988): 443–55.

Pope, Randolph. "Benet, Faulkner, and Bergson's Memory." Manteiga et al. 111–19.

——. "Historia y novela en la posguerra española." *Siglo XX/20th Century* 5.1–2 (1987–88): 16–24.

——. "Luis Goytisolo's *Antagonía* and Radical Change." *Anales de la Literatura Española Contemporánea* 13 (1988): 105–17.

"Prefacio." *Arbor* 1.3 (1944): n.p.

Proust, Marcel. *Remembrance of Things Past*. Trans. C. K. Scott Moncrieff, Terence Kilmartin, and Andreas Mayor. 3 vols. New York: Random House, 1981.

Quiñonero, Juan Pedro. "Entrevista con Carlos Castilla del Pino." *Informaciones de Artes y Letras* 95 (1970): 1.

"Revisión historiográfica del realismo social en España." Special issue of *Cuadernos Interdisciplinarios de Estudios Literarios* 4 (1993).

Ricoeur, Paul. "The Metaphorical Process as Cognition, Imagination, and Feeling." Sacks 141–57.

————. *The Rule of Metaphor.* Trans. Robert Czerny with Kathleen McLaughlin and John Costello. Toronto: U of Toronto P, 1977.

————. *Time and Narrative.* Trans. Kathleen Blamey and David Pellauer. 3 vols. Chicago: U of Chicago P, 1984–88.

Río, Angel del, and M. J. Benardete, eds. *El concepto contemporáneo de España.* Buenos Aires: Editorial Losado, 1946.

Roberts, Gemma. "La culpa y la búsqueda de la autenticidad en *San Camilo, 1936.*" *Novelistas españoles de postguerra.* Ed. Rodolfo Cardona. Madrid: Taurus, 1976. 205–18.

Robinson, Douglas. *American Apocalypses.* Baltimore: Johns Hopkins UP, 1985.

Rodríguez Puértolas, Julio. *Literatura fascista española.* 2 vols. Madrid: AKAL, 1987.

Rorty, Richard. *Philosophy and the Mirror of Nature.* Oxford: Oxford UP, 1980.

Sacks, Sheldon, ed. *On Metaphor.* Chicago: U of Chicago P, 1979.

Sánchez Albornoz, Claudio. *España, un enigma histórico.* 2 vols. Buenos Aires: Editorial Sudamericana, 1956.

Sánchez Montes, Juan. "Una revisión actual de las ideas sobre la decadencia española." *Arbor* 12.40 (1949): 613–17.

Sanz Villanueva, Santos. *Tendencias de la novela española actual.* Madrid: Cuadernos para el Diálogo, 1972.

Schaff, Adam. *History and Truth.* Oxford: Pergamon, 1976.

Schama, Simon. *Dead Certainties.* New York: Knopf, 1991.

Scholes, Robert. *Fabulation and Metafiction.* Urbana: U of Illinois P, 1979.

Seamon, Roger. "Narrative Practice and the Theoretical Distinction between History and Fiction." *Genre* 16 (1983): 197–218.

"Semprún lucha contra el olvido." *El País* 18 Sept. 1989: 19.

Servodidio, Mirella, and Marcia Welles, eds. *From Fiction to Metafiction: Essays in Honor of Carmen Martín Gaite.* Lincoln, Neb.: Society of Spanish and Spanish-American Studies, 1983.

Six, Abigail Lee. "Breaking Rules, Making History: A Postmodern Reading of Historiography in Juan Goytisolo's Fiction." D'haen and Bertens 33–60.

————. *Juan Goytisolo: The Case for Chaos.* New Haven: Yale UP, 1990.

Smith, Barbara Herrnstein. *On the Margins of Discourse.* Chicago: U of Chicago P, 1978.

Sobejano, Gonzalo. *Novela española de nuestro tiempo.* 2nd ed. Madrid: Editorial Prensa Española, 1975.

————. "Ante la novela de los años setenta." *Insula* 396–397 (Nov.–Dec. 1979): 1, 22.

————. "La novela ensimismada (1980–1985)." *España Contemporánea* 1 (1988): 9–26.

————. "Novela y metanovela en España." *Insula* 512–513 (Aug.–Sept. 1989): 4–7.

Soldevila-Durante, Ignacio. *La novela desde 1936.* Madrid: Alhambra, 1980.

————. "Esfuerzo titánico de la novela histórica." *Insula* 512–513 (Aug.–Sept. 1989): 8.

WORKS CITED

Sontag, Susan. "The Aesthetics of Silence." *A Susan Sontag Reader*. Harmondsworth, Eng.: Penguin, 1983. 181–204.

Spires, Robert. *Beyond the Metafictional Mode*. Lexington: UP of Kentucky, 1984.

——. "Juan Benet's Poetics of Open Spaces." Manteiga et al. 1–7.

——. "Mensaje social del discurso franquista en *Juan sin tierra, El cuarto de atrás* y *Teoría del conocimiento*." *Cuadernos Interdisciplinarios de Estudios Literarios* 4 (1993): 133–42.

——. "A Play of Difference: Fiction After Franco." *Letras Peninsulares* 1 (1988): 285–98.

Stevens, Wallace. "Asides on the Oboe." *The Collected Poems of Wallace Stevens*. New York: Knopf, 1957.

Suevos, Jesús. "España como unidad de destino. *Arbor* 40.151–52 (1958): 323–30.

Thomas, Hugh. *The Spanish Civil War*. New York: Harper Colophon, 1963.

Torrente Ballester, Gonzalo. *Fragmentos de apocalipsis*. Barcelona: Destino, 1977.

——. *La isla de los jacintos cortados*. Barcelona: Destino, 1980.

——. *Nuevos cuadernos de La Romana*. Barcelona: Destino, 1976.

——. *La rosa de los vientos*. Barcelona: Destino, 1985.

Tuñón de Lara, Manuel. *Metodología de la historia social de España*. Madrid: Siglo XXI, 1973.

——. "Pórtico: Primero de abril de 1939." García Delgado xi–xii.

——. "Problemas actuales de la historiografía española." *Sistema* 1 (1973): 31–50.

——, and José Antonio Biescas. *España bajo la dictadura franquista*. Barcelona: Labor, 1980.

Ugarte, Michael. "Juan Goytisolo: Unruly Disciple of Américo Castro." *Journal of Spanish Studies: Twentieth Century* 7 (1979): 353–64.

——. *Trilogy of Treason*. Columbia: U of Missouri P, 1982.

Ullman, P. L. "Sobre la rectificación surrealista del espejo emblemático en *San Camilo, 1936*." *Neophilologus* 66 (1982): 377–85.

Valls Montes, R. *La interpretación de la historia de España y sus orígenes ideológicos en el bachillerato franquista, 1938–1953*. Valencia, Sp.: Universidad de Valencia, 1983.

Vicens Vives, Jaime. *Approaches to the History of Spain*. Trans. John C. Ulman. Berkeley: U of California P, 1970.

——. *Aproximación a la historia de España*. 2nd ed. Barcelona: Editorial Vicens-Vives, 1960.

Villanueva, Darío. *'El Jarama' de Sánchez Ferlosio. Su estructura y significado*. Santiago, Sp.: Universidad de Santiago de Compostela, 1973.

——. "Novela lírica, novela poemática." *Insula* 512–513 (Aug.–Sept. 1989): 7–8.

Weinsheimer, Joel. *Gadamer's Hermeneutics*. New Haven: Yale UP, 1985.

Weinstein, Mark A. "The Creative Imagination in Fiction and History." *Genre* 9 (1976): 263–77.

White, Hayden. *The Content of the Form*. Baltimore: Johns Hopkins UP, 1987.

WORKS CITED

——. *Metahistory.* Baltimore: Johns Hopkins UP, 1973.

——. *Tropics of Discourse.* Baltimore: Johns Hopkins UP, 1978.

Wilde, Oscar. "The Decay of Lying." *The Artist as Critic: Critical Writings of Oscar Wilde,* ed. Richard Ellman. New York: Random House, 1968. 290–319.

Williams, William Carlos. *Paterson.* New York: New Directions, 1963.

Zamora, Lois Park. *Writing the Apocalypse.* Cambridge: Cambridge UP, 1989.

WORKS CITED

Index

10, 90–92, 102; and fiction, 2–14;
and Francoism, 1–3, 9–12, 15–38;
heroic concept of, 46–47, 74–75,
123–24, 133–34, 159 n.7; and multiple meanings, 107–11, 123–26;
and myth, 11, 33–34, 86; and post-
Francoism, 152–56; and postmodernism, 5, 8, 10, 13, 117–19; and
time, 7, 22, 32–33, 36; universal
concept of, 25–30. *See also* Novel
of memory; Social Realism

Ilie, Paul, 165 n.3
Intertextuality, 78–84, 126–28. *See
also* Postmodernism
Isabel la Católica, 35, 48, 69–70

James, Henry, 39, 59
Jameson, Fredric, 118
Jordan, Barry, 11
Joyce, James, 139–41

Kermode, Frank, 34, 61, 146

Labanyi, Jo, 11, 35, 147–48, 165–66
n.5
Laín Entralgo, Pedro, 18, 22
Language, 62–64, 80–82, 93, 100,
103, 107–11, 117, 121–22, 128, 130,
137–43, 149–50. *See also* Postmod-
ernism
Las dos Españas, 29
Levin, Harry, 45
Lévi-Strauss, Claude, 17
Lyotard, François, 132, 151

Major, Clarence, 122
Maltby, Paul, 139
Mangini, Shirley, 10, 43, 46
Marichal, Juan, 31
Marsé, Juan, 42

Martín Gaite, Carmen: *El cuarto de
atrás,* 69–72, 82–83, 105, 140, 161
n.2
Memory. *See* Novel of memory
Menéndez Pidal, Ramón, 24
Menéndez y Pelayo, Marcelino, 21–
26, 30–32
Mink, Louis, 4, 25
Montero Díaz, Santiago, 46–47
Morán, Fernando, 11, 46, 55, 161 n.5
Morse, Jonathan, 68, 81
Munz, Peter, 56
Myth, 11, 33–34, 86, 97, 115, 133–34,
146–48. *See also* History

New Historicism, 8–9
Nietzsche, Friedrich, 91, 97, 106, 121,
165 n.9
Novel of memory, 12, 66–86, 117, 120–
21, 161–62 n.1, 163 n.2; characteris-
tics of, 66–69. *See also* Benet, Juan;
Goytisolo, Juan; Goytisolo, Luis;
Martín Gaite, Carmen

Palacio Atard, Vicente, 20–21, 25,
28–29, 33
Paniker, Raimundo, 17
Pasamar Alzuria, Gonzalo, 17–18,
20–21, 24
Payne, Stanley, 31
Pérez Embid, Florentino, 17–18, 21,
23, 31
Pius XII, 18
Pope, Randolph, 23–24
Post-Francoist Spain, 152–56
Posthistory, 37
Postmodernism, 5, 116–43; and lan-
guage, 117–18, 121–22, 142–43.
See also Cela, Camilo José;
Goytisolo, Juan; History; Torrente
Ballester, Gonzalo

INDEX

David K. Herzberger is Professor
of Spanish and Comparative Literature at
the University of Connecticut.

Library of Congress Cataloging-in-Publication Data

Herzberger, David K.
Narrating the past : fiction and historiography
in postwar Spain / David K. Herzberger.
p.   cm.
Includes bibliographical references and index.
ISBN 0-8223-1582-3. — ISBN 0-8223-1597-1 (pbk.)
1. Spanish fiction—20th century—History and criticism.
2. Literature and history—Spain.   3. Historiography—Spain.
4. Spain—History—20th century—Historiography.   I. Title.
PQ6144.H47   1995
863'.6409358—dc20   94-24973   CIP